Learning Together

Keeping Teachers and Students Actively Involved in Learning by Writing Across the Curriculum

A SOURCEBOOK OF IDEAS AND WRITING EXERCISES

By Dr. Theodore Panitz

NEW FORUMS PRESS INC.

Stillwater, Oklahoma U.S.A.

Contents

Preface

Writing is an evolutionary process whereby the author revises his/her ideas, values and approaches, not just a mechanical act of placing words in a correct sequence with appropriate grammar. It is intensely personal and interactive with the subject matter, whether in the form of a brief "One-Minute Paper" at the end of class, a five-minute summary during class, an extended essay, or research paper.

The purpose of this book is to provide a wide range of examples of writing across the curriculum (WAC) activities in order to encourage teachers to use writing in their classes regularly as a way of stimulating critical thinking in their students and providing variety in their teaching methods.

Over the years I have developed a substantial number of writing assignments for a variety of courses including engineering, and developmental and college mathematics. Writing this book has helped me focus my ideas about WAC and to put all my writing assignments in one place for review and use by other teachers. The book itself illustrates the value of writing in that my ideas about what should be included continue to evolve as I write.

Why is writing an important part of any pedagogy? Research is clear that writing causes the author to think critically and deeply about the topic under consideration, often evaluating and rethinking one's beliefs and values. From the student's perspective writing develops communication skills and problem-solving abilities needed in today's workplace. It makes learning more meaningful by relating student's personal experiences to the course material and generates course ownership through creative writing by personalizing it. From a teacher's perspective writing helps build rapport between teacher and student by opening a variety of communication approaches, by including students in the evaluation and application of course information, and through its inclusion with collaborative learning exercises.

How This Book is Organized

This book is presented in three sections. The first presents reasons why WAC is important to all classes, not just English classes. It is hoped that this section will serve to encourage new WAC users by highlighting and explaining the many benefits created by WAC. The second section gives detailed descriptions of 29 different writing assignments the author has developed, which have been tested in a variety of courses. Section 3 provides a listing of world wide web sites which have interesting materials concerning WAC approaches with numerous links to colleges and universities.

The assignments are organized into five categories: Motivational-General, Personal Reflection/Motivation, Group/Processing, Content/Personal Reflection, and Content/Enhancing. Each category is intended to solicit responses which will foster student motivation by having students look at personal issues facing them or through examination of content, or procedures. For example, in assignment #1D students are asked to analyze the "Seven Principles Of Good Education" and make suggestions as to how they might be applied to the course. This is done at the beginning of the semester to call attention to the value of their active participation in the class as well as the nature of teaching and learning.

Each writing assignment description is divided into six sections. The first is a description of the background and rationale for the assignment plus additional observations which are intended to be helpful to the reader in anticipating the kinds of responses students may give. The second section highlights the purposes and benefits expected from the assignment. The third section suggests alternative uses and ways of modifying the assignment to meet special needs of different classes. The fourth section suggests applications and procedures for using the assignment to generate cooperative learning opportunities in and out of class. The fifth section includes a sample assignment which may be modified by individual instructors to meet their particular needs or interests. The sixth section presents samples of student responses to the assignment. This section is unique to this book and is intended to help instructors anticipate the types of student responses they may receive.

Perhaps the best way to use this book is to browse through section two to see what interests you, versus reading it from beginning to end. It is intended for three very different audiences. First it is for teachers who already use WAC and are comfortable with this approach but would like to explore new methods and ideas. For beginning teachers, reading through the detailed descriptions presented in Chapter 2 would be helpful to build a foundation and basis for using WAC plus these materials provide sample assignments and student responses. For the novice WAC user reading through the detailed descriptions would be most helpful with the idea in mind of finding one or two new options to add to their portfolio of WAC assignments.

Readers are encouraged to explore the wide variety of WAC materials available on the WWW and in this book with an eye toward developing their own unique applications and assignments. As stated earlier, the WAC process is an active one providing a high degree of creativity and innovation. Introduction of WAC into courses has the potential to stimulate both student and teacher interest in course content and to encourage new approaches to learning and teaching.

Why Use Writing Assignments in Courses Other Than English Composition?

The eternal question raised by students, "Why do I need to do writing assignments in this course, it is not an English course?" has many answers. Assigning writing exercises in courses like Physics, Calculus, biology, etc., may indeed seem strange to students because in these courses information transfer appears to be the primary teaching technique. In reality our job as teachers is to create an environment that encourages students' to take responsibility for understanding underlying concepts and to enable them to solve new as well as existing problems.

Some of the reasons for using WAC methods presented below may be more meaningful to students while others will receive a more empathetic response from professors. All of the reasons for using writing in college classes, however, speak to the heart and philosophy or Writing Across the Curriculum (WAC); helping students become active, independent learners.

The following reasons for using WAC in non-English courses are presented to help convince professors and students of the value and need for using this paradigm. They are not intended to be exhaustive. Hopefully other ideas will occur to readers as they peruse the ideas presented below.

In addition, WAC is not meant to be an exclusive paradigm but one tool of many used by instructors to build critical thinking skills in students. WAC is especially effective when used with collaborative learning techniques or in large lectures to help focus students attention on a particular topic or assess their understanding of material being discussed. Informal writing, outlined in Section 3 of this book, highlights the value of WAC in personalizing instruction when using any teaching paradigm.

Writing helps the author evolve in his/her thinking. Boyer (1987), Zinsser (1985)

Writing causes authors to evolve in their thinking by reflecting on ideas, gathering new information, modifying their thoughts and/or philosophy or approach to a subject (such as teaching) through the process of writing, editing and rewriting. According to Bean (1996), "The underlying premise is that writing is closely linked with thinking and that in presenting students with significant problems to write about–and in creating an environment that demands their best writing–we can promote their general cognitive and intellectual growth. When we make students struggle with their writing we are making them struggle with thought itself" (p. xiii).

Naisbitt and Aburdene (1985) make an even stronger case for writing to promote thinking. They say, "If our students' thinking skills have deteriorated badly–and we know they have–perhaps it is because their writing skills have grown equally slack.

More and more educators have reached the same conclusion and come up with the same solution: strengthen the writing curriculum as an avenue to sharpen thinking" (p. 152).

This book provides an excellent personal example. I started out with the idea of writing a short "what-to-write" book by presenting and explaining writing assignments which I have developed and tested in my classes. I have expanded it to include a section on helpful internet world wide web pages and reasons for using writing. I expect that even after I finish the final rewrite of this book I will continue to evolve in my understanding and presentation of WAC materials.

Writing generates critical thinking.

At a minimum writing improves the author's critical thinking skills. One's ability to solve problems, to examine ideas carefully and support them from evidence, and the ability to incorporate and synthesize information are all enhanced through formal and informal writing activities. Formal writing especially and informal writing to a lessor degree requires organizational skills, vocabulary, philosophical underpinnings, and determination, to be successful. The process of rewriting and editing is time consuming and requires hard work. The process of thinking is very physically demanding as well as mentally. WAC programs build these characteristics in students over time.

Bean (1996) presents the essence of critical thinking through his review of Dewey's explanation of critical thinking. "Although definitions in the pedagogical literature vary in detail, in their broad outlines they are largely elaborations, extensions, and refinements of the progressive views of John Dewey (1916), who rooted critical thinking in the student's engagement with a problem. "The most significant question which can be asked," says Dewey. "About any situation or experience proposed to induce learning is what quality of problem it involves" (p. 182). Problems, for Dewey, evoke student's natural curiosity and stimulate both learning and critical thought," (Bean p. 2).

Personalizes college classes.

Large lecture classes are notoriously impersonal. Students rarely interact with the lecturer during class. One way for a professor to personalize a class is to use informal writing assignments which are usually of a personal nature. Students may be asked to reflect upon their performance in the class, problems or successes they are having and their views of class procedures and methods. These assignments are usually not graded in order to encourage the students to be open about their reactions and feelings. Contact is made more personal in lecture classes because the students are able to communicate directly with the instructor through writing assignments. The teacher has an opportunity to respond to the student either in writing or in person, thus opening lines of communication which make any class more personal.

Bean (1996) makes a strong case for combining writing with collaborative exercises in large lecture classes. He states, "A second advantage of the method described here (use of collaborative groups) can be adapted to large classes, even in lecture halls where students have to turn around in their seats to form groups. Whereas it is nearly impossible to lead a whole-class discussion in a room of two hundred students, it is entirely possible in a large class to give students a critical thinking task, have students work with their neighbors for ten minutes or so, and then ask representative groups to present or justify their solutions," (p 151).

Builds rapport between teacher and student.

Students often report that they do better in classes and feel more motivated when they feel the teacher is taking a personal interest in their performance. As discussed above, opening a two-way line of communication between the student and instructor personalizes courses and this enables teachers to build a rapport with their students. Students and teachers may share experiences with each other, explain their rationale for class activities, provide suggestions for assistance, among the many possible interactions which tend humanize the author of an informal writing assignment.

Brufee (1993) summarizes the effect of having the teacher and students read each other's work. He states, "Reading one another's work and listening to one another's work read aloud gives students confidence in the value of their own words and ideas, because they learn that other writers are interested in what they have to say. Learning what their peers are interested in, furthermore, they get to know one another at a level of intellectual engagement, in many cases for the first time. And they become increasingly sensitive to triviality, excessive generality, and errors in usage and logic," (p. 61).

Sibley (1990) has articulated a benefit for the teacher. He States "My chief reward from these papers is seeing them (students) learning mathematics and learning how to learn. Next comes the pleasure of reading interesting papers, especially on topics new to me. The more mathematically ambitious students come more frequently to consult with me, giving me a chance to know students who sometimes have no need to seek help," (p. 53).

Opens communication between students and professors.

Students are often hesitant to approach a professor regarding personal problems, difficulties with a course or just to meet socially. This may be due in part to the nature of the professor, as viewed by the student, as someone in a position above them either intellectually or structurally. Likewise students find it difficult to make friends in classes, especially large lecture classes where there is little interaction. Writing initiates the process of communicating between people. By sharing writing efforts, peer editing, and group writing students get to know each other better and through informal writing students open many lines of communication.

White explains his procedures and results in math classes. "Now I let them write about almost anything the want in their paragraphs (it should have some relevance to the statement at hand): subjective responses, paraphrases of the statement and/or proof, conjectures of corollaries or generalizations, discussions, alternate proofs. Questions about the mathematics that trouble them, gripes about the course and even (shudder!) gripes about me. This opens a marvelous two-way channel of communication between the instructor and each student. I collect the journals three time a term,

---

read them carefully and return them promptly. I try to answer their questions and address their concerns in writing in their journals. I know I learn much more about each of them by their journals than I would otherwise," (p. 36).

Creates variety in the pedagogy of a course.

Whether a course is taught using a lecture approach, which is primarily information oriented, or collaboratively, which is more student centered and interactive, writing always provides an alternative approach. Sipka (1990) points out that "Many benefits of writing can be accepted as axioms. For example, writing (especially in-class writing) assignments add variety to the typical lecture oriented math class," (p. 13). Writing may be done in class as short informal assignments, or longer multi step activities done individually or collaboratively during a longer segment of a class. The product of each writing activity may then be used as the basis for a whole class discussion or consideration by groups working together. Follow up homework assignments may also be derived from in class writing or out of class assignments may be started in class. Short One Minute Paper type activities used at any time during a class can help the instructor determine whether students understand the material being covered or gain information on their reactions to class procedures. There are as many varieties as there are potential assignments. Neither the lecture or collaborative learning should be used exclusively as a course pedagogy. A good mix of the two plus the liberal use of writing makes for interesting and exciting classes.

Develops communication skills needed by today's workforce.

In survey after survey today's employers indicate they want employees who have good written and oral communication skills, strong problem solving abilities, and a high degree of motivation. Houp and Pearsall (1984) researched the central role communications have in the technical professions. The found that engineers spend 24% of their week writing and 34% of their time reading other people's writing. The engineers surveyed felt that writing helped them get promoted and figured in their evaluation of subordinates when recommending them for advancement. Faires and Nelson (1990) state "After all, if they can't negotiate their native language, how can they be entrusted with the greater responsibilities associated with more complex and ambitious assignments. How well graduates write and speak affects their professional credibility," (p. 42).

Training in the writing requirement is an obvious by-product of WAC, The problem solving comes from developing critical thinking skills which are associated with good writing, i.e. good organization, decision making based on sound information, writing and rewriting until one is satisfied with the result, peer editing, meeting deadlines, etc. Good writing skills are even reflected in the layout and information presented in a resume; the first sample of writing a perspective employer sees. The standards proposed by the AMATYC highlights the benefit of writing in math: "As students learn to speak and write about mathematics, they develop a mathematical power and become better prepared to use mathematics beyond the classroom," (p. 11). This applies to all academic areas as well as mathematics.

Practicing writing improves writing. (Rose 1990)

The cliche "Practice makes perfect" is most applicable here. Many students find writing well thought out, coherent papers to be very difficult. Perhaps part of the reason may stem from the fact that they do not get many opportunities to practice either formal or informal writing in classes other than English courses. Students are generally required to take a year of English composition courses where the writing is intense. After that exposure little formal writing follows so students get stale from lack of practice. Critical thinking skills need to be developed and continually reinforced to be available to the student over time.

Sibley highlights the benefit of practice through collaborative student writing efforts when he points out that "The students may benefit in multiple ways from referring. First they become more sensitive to the need for clear writing as they scrutinize their peers' writing. Second they learn the content of other students' papers. Third, the students make valuable comments on aspects I never noticed. Fourth, the student readers provide a supportive audience. Every paper benefits noticeably from rewriting," (p. 53).

Writing involves students directly in the learning process.

Kenney (1990) makes the case that "Writing, of course, is the vehicle of language in which we are most interested in here, especially as it affects and involves learning. In particular, writing promotes student-centered learning." In addition he states "Writing promotes student ownership of an idea primarily in the following ways: first, by writing, a student puts ideas into his or her own words; and second, through the process of writing, a student gradually makes an idea his own, makes it part of the architecture of his or her own knowledge," (p. 17).

Writing is a hands on, active, and in some cases interactive activity. Formal content oriented writing requires students to develop a thorough understanding of the underlying concepts in order to write about them. Research or in depth reading of the text is necessary for students to formulate opinions or follow the author's reasoning. The very fact that writing is a physical activity separates it from listening to lectures or student discussions and makes it an active process versus passive. The call to write is a call to action both mentally and physically.

When completing a writing assignment students need to decide what material will be included, what order of presentation will be used, what style or genre will be employed, how much background research they will need to do to become proficient in the subject matter, to name a few of the decisions they will need to make which directly involves them in establishing a learning process.

Brandeau describes how a student benefited from journal writing in a math class. "The journal process described above has enriched Allen's understanding of mathematics in a way very different from other forms of teaching and learning. The process personalized the mathematics. It required him to get actively involved, engaged, often lost in the problems he was trying to solve. Allen has been involved in making his own meaning of what he was doing," (p. 75).

Helps people operate at a higher level of abstraction. Fulwiler (1982)

Writing involves the use of symbols (words) to express an author's ideas much as mathematicians use letters and symbols to represent operations and concepts. Expressing one's ideas in symbols requires a highly trained mind because of the abstract nature of the communication form. Writing often enables one to express ideas through analogies and indirect explanations. This too represents a higher level of thinking. Abstract thinking requires the use of higher order brain functions such as awareness of spatial relations and interrelations between concepts. Practicing writing builds these brain functions.

Foster to improvement requires persistent and frequent contact with students in and out of class.

The process of writing is not an isolated one where students function independently and competitively. Quite the contrary, writing involves multiple cycles of peer brainstorming, peer editing, consultation with the instructor and rewrites before a finished product is completed. Student-teacher conferences should be a major element in any writing program to insure extensive communication about the student's progress during any writing assignment. A secondary benefit to using writing conferences is that it helps build a rapport between teacher and student through a reciprocal familiarity. This can be time consuming and requires a commitment by both the student and professor which is well rewarded by increases student motivation and improvement throughout a semester.

WAC exercises make learning more meaningful by relating the student's experiences to the course material, generating ownership through creative writing by personalizing it.

Informal writing assignments provide an excellent opportunity for students to write about their personal experiences in relation to course topics or concepts. Exercises such as writing an autobiography in relation to the course, a short story, or a letter to the editor, etc., require students to consider course materials from their personal perspective. Adult education research has shown that when people relate course materials to personal experiences they retain more information and are able to apply course concepts much better. Writing helps formalize this process by asking students to document and sometimes defend their views and personal philosophies, based on their real life experiences.

Bean (1996) emphasizes the idea that tasks which link course concepts to students' personal experiences or previously existing knowledge "help students assimilate new concepts by connecting the concepts to personal experiences. As cognitive research has shown (Norman 1980), to assimilate a new concept, learners must link it back to a structure of known material, determining how a new concept is both similar to and different from what the learner already knows," (p. 123).

Helps students join the academic society (community) of their choice through the acquisition of vocabulary and learning about the new culture's norms.

Bruffee (1993) identified the process by which students enter academic fields as involving the acquisition of the vocabulary of the particular field of interest and an understanding of the new culture's norms through interactions and discussions with fellow students and the instructor via collaborative activities. Writing is an important component of the process because it provides a basis for student interactions and a method for students to explore the norms of the new academic community. Defending contrary views, debating issues, formulating opinions about concepts, editing peer's work and teaching one's peers all lead to higher order thinking skills and a more thorough understanding of the material under study. Brufee observes that "Every time we write, we try to construct, reconstruct, or conserve knowledge by justifying our beliefs to each other socially. We judge what we write, and other people judge it, according to assumptions, goals, values, rules, and conventions of these communities," (p. 55).

Keith (1990) underscores the idea of students joining new learning communities through the use of language and writing when she states, "They (writing assignments) allow students to read and process the writing of other students, and they allow students to 'talk' mathematics with more ease, and to develop a language for asking questions," (p. 6). She continues, "The in class evaluation of writing assignments stimulates meaningful discussions of mathematics as a language and strategies for learning it. The assignments break down fear in the classroom, and nurture a more open environment for asking questions," (p. 7).

Writing can be made user friendly through informal writing. Bean (1996)

Formal writing such as term papers and essays can be discouraging to the novice or beginning writer; they take a high degree of expertise and experience to be done well. Students need more practice with types of writing which are less structured and less evaluation oriented in terms of grading. Informal writing may as vigorous and time consuming as formal assignments, however, the purpose is significantly different. Journal writing for example has many uses, including note taking, text summary, student observations about the course or personal reflections on their performance, review of course materials to name a few. The one minute paper may be used to ask students to comment on their understanding of class material either during or at the end of the class and to reflect on what questions they still have. These assignments establish a philosophy that writing is appropriate throughout the course both inside and outside of class with the primary purpose to encourage students to write frequently in order to continually practice and build their thinking and writing skills.

Writing is synergistic with collaborative groups.

Abercrombie (1960) worked with medical students at the University Hospital in London. She concluded that her students learned diagnostic skills better if they were placed in independent groups to address a diagnostic problem. The use of small groups did not just lead to a pooling of knowledge but the collaborative approach promoted argumentation and consensus building where each student had to support a hypothesis with reasons and evidence in an attempt to sway the others. Keith (1990) uses collaborative activities in math classes and concludes, "When students work in groups in creative activities, they go further, and are encouraged to think of mathematics as a collaborative subject," (p. 9). When the two concepts are combined, collaboration and writing, the effect is to create even stronger critical thinking skills and oral and written presentation skills by the students.

Students participate in the evaluation and application of course information Rose. (1990)

The one minute paper provides an excellent example of how writing may be use to encourage students to evaluate the course on an ongoing basis and communicate to the instructor their progress and understanding of course concepts. Questions asked in the one minute paper may be varied from "What did you learn today?" and "What questions remain in your mind?" to how students feel about class procedures, exam structures and schedules or virtually any aspect of the class. Instructors must be willing to address student concerns for this form of writing to be effective. This may be done by the instructor writing back in response to specific students questions or comments, involving the class in a discussion about concerns raised, or through communicating one's rationale for a particular exercise or class procedure. Students are empowered and become motivated when instructors ask for their observations and respond positively.

Keith (1990) observes that writing assignments "provide the instructor with an open window on where the class stands, and immediate feedback on how to teach the problems of the class or where reteaching is necessary, prior to an exam," (p. 6). Kenney further states that "Students' opinions on how their education is progressing are seldom solicited, particularly in these days of the return to the "core curriculum," which largely ignores the issue of student empowerment. Students must believe they are active participants in the academic arena if they are to avoid the passive receptor syndrome," (p. 20).

WAC stimulates creativity through brainstorming activities.

A natural starting point for any writing activity involves group brainstorming about the topic(s) under consideration for a particular assignment. Very creative exercises may be used to help generate ideas for stories, essays and even term projects. Many people think of writing as an accumulation of facts which need to placed in an orderly fashion to make of defend a thesis. Critical thinking involves much more creativity than such a mechanical approach. Writers need to be trained in creativity activities and be given lots of opportunities to practice. Short, informal writing assignments provide an excellent medium for students to build their creative thinking abilities and skills.

Bean (1996) observes that "Small group tasks can also be used in conjunction with formal writing assignments to help students brainstorm ideas for an upcoming essay, discover and rehearse arguments, or critique rough drafts. In these cases, the small group task promotes exploration of ideas needed for the essay," (p. 152). The Curriculum and Evaluation Standards for School Mathematics (NCTM) (1989) states, "The simple exercise of writing an explanation of how a problem was solved not only helps clarify a student's thinking but also may provide other students fresh insights gained from viewing the problem from a new perspective" (p. 142).

Writing in different genres creates different ways of thinking.

Writing poetry, a short story, fiction or nonfiction works,

requires different ways of thinking and approaching each type of writing. By exposing students to many different genres and asking them to write in these styles we expand their horizons and increase their critical thinking skills. Asking students to review different genres also exposes them to different approaches to thinking and presentation of information. This is accomplished through English Composition courses, but rarely in non-English based courses. Asking students to write a poem about a math concept or their reaction to math can have a cathartic effect as this type of informal writing assignment encourages students to delve into their hearts and express their concerns and gratification. Having students write a short story about a math of science concept often releases a creative potential which helps students understand that concept much better.

Helps clarify one's goals and values.

According to Brufee (1993) "Every time we write, we try to construct, reconstruct, or conserve knowledge by justifying our beliefs to each other socially. We judge what we write, and other people judge it, according to the assumptions, goals, values, rules, and conventions of these communities," (p. 55). By choosing writing assignments which encourage students to present alternate points of view and argue for opposing positions we challenge their views of their existing values and either cause them to rethink those values or strengthen their positions through a well thought out explanation. Bean (1996) makes the case that ".... students come to college imagining knowledge as the acquisition of correct information rather than the ability, say, to stake out and support a position in a complex conversation. Eventually, students develop a complex view of knowledge, where individuals have to take a stand in the light of their own values and the best available reasons and evidence" (p. 25).

Scientific knowledge is constructed through conversation and writing.

Students aspiring to enter the science or mathematics communities especially need to be able to communicate through writing in the form of papers for refereed journals, presentations at conferences and book publishing. This is how they create new knowledge; by communicating with each other and exposing their ideas to intense scrutiny and evaluation. It takes a great deal of practice to become proficient at writing for technical readers. The best place to start is in technical college courses as well as nontechnical courses.

According to Brufee (1993), "Writing is central even to the construction of scientific knowledge. In Laboratory of Life: The Social Construction of Scientific Facts (1986), Bruno Latour and Steve Woolgar show that scientists construct scientific knowledge through conversation, and that the most important kind of conversation scientists engage in is indirect, that is, displaced into writing," (p. 52). The scientific method models critical thinking processes used in writing. Kurfiss (1988) defines critical thinking as "an investigation whose purpose is to explore a situation, phenomenon, question, or problem to arrive at a hypothesis or conclusion about it that integrates all available information and that can therefore be convincingly justified," (p. 2). Bean (1996 p. 3) Brufee (1993) describes the writing of scientific texts as follows. "In generating texts-in writing- scientists do what all writers do who write in an active engaged community of knowledgeable peers. They carry on a meticulous sorting of weak connections between existing ideas by willingly subjecting themselves to mutual criticism. They read and reread, check and recheck, revise and re-revise their own and each other's written material" (p. 53).

References

Abercrombie, M.L.J., (1960), "The Anatomy of Judgment: Concerning the Processes of Perception, Communication, and Reasoning," London: Hutchinson

American Mathematical Association of Two Year Colleges, (1995) "Crossroads in Mathematics: Standards for Introductory College Mathematics Before Calculus"

Bean, J. C., (1996), "Engaging ideas: The professor's guide to integrating writing, critical thinking and active learning in the classroom," San Francisco, CA: Jossey Bass Inc.

Boyer, E., (1987), " College: The Undergraduate Experience in America," New York, NY: Harper and Row

Brandeau, L., (1990), "Rewriting Our Stories of Mathematics," in "Using Writing to Teach Mathematics- MAA Notes #16", Sterrett (Ed.) Mathematical Association of America

Brufee, K. A., (1993), "Collaborative Learning: Higher Education, Interdependence and the Authority of Knowledge," Baltimore, MD: The Johns Hopkins University Press

Dewey, J., (1916), Democracy In Education, New York, NY: Macmillan

Faires, J. D., Nelson, C. A., (1990), "Technical Writing for Mathematics Projects," in "Using Writing to Teach Mathematics- MAA notes #16" Sterrett (ed.), Mathematics Association of America

Fulwiler, T., (1982), "Writing as an Act of Cognition." In C. W. Griffin (Ed.) New Directions for teaching and Learning: Teaching Writing in all Disciplines, San Francisco: Jossey Bass Inc.

Houp, K., & Pearsall, T., (1984), "Reporting Technical Information," New York, NY: Macmillan

Keith, S. Z., (1990), "Writing for Educational Objectives in a Calculus Course." In "Using Writing to Teach Mathematics, MAA notes #16," Sterrett (Ed.), Mathematics Association of American

Kenney, E. A., (1990), "A Reply to Colleagues on Writing Across the Curriculum." In "Using Writing to Teach Mathematics, MAA notes #16," Sterrett (Ed.), Mathematical Association of America

Kurfiss, J. G., (1988), "Critical Thinking: Theory, Research, Practice and Possibilities," ASHE-ERIC Higher Education Report No. 2 Washington, D.C.: ERIC Clearinghouse on Higher education and the Association for the Study of Higher Education

Latour, B., & Woolgar, S., (1986), "Laboratory Life: The Construction of Scientific Facts," Princeton, NJ: Princeton UP

Naisbett, J. & Aburdeen, P., (1985), "Reinventing the Corporation," New York, NY: Warner

National Council of Teachers of Mathematics, (1989), "Mathematics Curriculum and Evaluation Standards for School Mathematics," Reston, VA

Norman, D. A., (1980), "What Goes On In the Mind Of the Learner." In W. J. McKeachie (ed.) "Learning, Cognition, and College Teaching, New Directions for Teaching and Learning," no. 2 San Francisco, CA: Jossey-Bass Inc.

Rose, B. J., (1990), "Using Expressive Writing to Support Mathematics Instruction: Benefits for Student, Teacher, Classroom," in "Using Writing to Teach Mathematics- MAA notes #16," Sterrett (ed.) Mathematical Association of America

Sibley, T., (1990), "Three R's for Mathematics Papers: 'Riting, Refereeing and Rewriting" in "Using Writing to Teach Mathematics- MAA notes #16," Sterrett (ed.), Mathematical Association of America

Sipka, T. (1990), "Writing in Mathematics: A Plethora of Possibilities," in "Using Writing to Teach Mathematics- MAA notes #16," Mathematical Association of America

White, A. (1990), "A Writing-Intensive Mathematics Course at Western Michigan University," in Using Writing to teach Mathematics- MAA notes #16," Mathematical Association of America

Zinsser, W., (1985), "On Writing Well," New York, NY: Harper and Row

TABLE OF CONTENTS OF WRITING EXERCISES

1-MOTIVATIONAL, GENERAL

How can we motivate students at the very beginning of our classes, encourage them to reflect upon their previous experiences and introduce a philosophical basis for our teaching methods? The five writing assignments presented in section 1 address these questions and more. By writing a letter to students prior to the beginning of class interest in their success is established and a method of communication is presented to them. Students can be encouraged to call the professor in advance if they have any problems or concerns about taking a particular course. Other assignments in this section encourage students to reflect upon their backgrounds, the nature of learning and teaching, and their role in the class. A success contract is included which emphasizes both the students and teachers' responsibilities during the semester.

A- Write a letter to your students prior to the beginning of the semester
B- Student autobiography- written prior to the beginning of class
C- Student profile for first class introductions
D- Analyzing the Seven Principles of Good Education
E- Student/Professor success contract

WRITE A LETTER TO YOUR STUDENTS PRIOR TO THE BEGINNING OF THE SEMESTER

Description

Imagine this scene. It is about two weeks prior to the beginning of the semester and your students are thinking about everything but their class with you or what lies ahead for them in the new term. They go to their mailboxes and find letter with your college's return address and your name above that. What a surprise! As they look through the materials they find a welcoming letter, a writing assignment (their math autobiography–WAC exercise #1) due at the first class and a course syllabus. They find the letter is less intimidating than they anticipated and is actually pretty humorous and it helps to allay their fears about math. They are assured that there will be help available from many sources including themselves and that this will be an interactive class which will encourage their participation during class.

Imagine their participation in the learning process. To end the letter there are two phone numbers, one for your office and one for your home. The students are encouraged to call if they have any questions or concerns.

Most, but not all, students react very positively to this outreach effort. Those who are concerned will call to clarify exactly what is expected of them and what their roles will be in the class. Some students call just because they have been encouraged to do so and like the idea of talking to a teacher before the semester starts.

The letter sets a tone of high expectations by giving the students an assignment prior to the first class, suggesting that they get the text and read the first chapter, and by outlining how much time will be needed for success in the course. By its very nature the letter signifies that this class will not be a typical math class where the students simply come and listen to a lecture and then go off to fend for themselves. It establishes the collaborative nature of the learning process as the paradigm which will be followed in the course. For those students who feel this approach may be inappropriate for them it gives them an opportunity to discuss their concerns prior to class directly with the professor and to make course changes if their concerns are not ameliorated.

When I first started using this technique I was very concerned that students would misunderstand the intent or overreact to the pre-class assignment. Discussions with students in the first class have shown me that their reactions are quite positive and the letter raises the students expectations about the positive nature of the class. Students are impressed that I would take the time to communicate with them and encourage them even before we met for the first time.

Purposes and Benefits

1. To grab students' attention prior to the beginning of the course in order to emphasize the serious but user friendly nature of the class.

2. To set high expectations for both the students and the teacher to make the class interesting and enjoyable.

3. To ease student's math anxiety through humor and a description of the help available throughout the institution.

4. To demonstrate my interest in writing across the curriculum. If I am going to ask them to write in a math class then it is important for me to demonstrate my writing style and effort.

5. To communicate the time requirements needed for success in the course.

6. To introduce students to the professor prior to class: encourage communication between them.

7. To alert students to the interactive nature of the class, through the use of collaborative learning techniques, and the many other interactive approaches which will be used throughout the semester. This letter initiates the process.

Alternate Uses

1. Convey your expectations for the course and course prerequisites or other requirements.

2. Ask students to reflect on their goals for the course, their career objectives, or reasons for attending your institution.

3. Request students be prepared for first class activities such as pairs interviewing/reporting or other warm up activities which may require preparation.

4. Send students materials to be used in the first class.

5. Send students materials to introduce the course such as newspaper articles, research papers etc.

Implications/Applications for Collaborative Learning Opportunities

1. The letter creates an interactive environment by inviting students to call the professor prior to class.

2. In asking the students to write their math autobiography they will be prepared for the first class warm-up/collaborative activity where students interview each other and report back to the whole class about their partner.

3. In the pair-interview-report exercise students are asked to determine how their partner feels about math and what their biggest concern is. This leads to a class discussion about math anxiety, a very common problem.

4. The letter highlights the positive nature of groups and benefits of helping each other to succeed in the course.

5. Other materials may be included which describe the class procedures thus preparing students for the interactive nature of the class.

Dear Elementary Algebra Student,

Welcome to the Fall of 1995 and Elementary Algebra. I can't think of a better way to spend a Spring semester, having fun with algebra. I would like to say hello and offer a few words of advice and encouragement before we meet on Sept. 6. I promise not to use more than 5 x 10 words in this letter. The prerequisite for this course is DE-051 Basic Math an identifiable pulse and a temperature of 98.6F and permission from your psychiatrist to subject yourself to this course over the next 15 weeks with this instructor, alias Attilla the teacher.

I have a few suggestions that are intended to guarantee your success in this course. If you make a good effort there is no doubt in my mind that you will pass. I am batting 1000 so far. (What the heck does batting 1000 mean?)

1. It is vitally, imperatively, critically important that you read the text BEFORE class and TRY TO DO as many exercises as is humanly possible.

The text is "Elementary/intermediate algebra," by Aufmann and Barker. Get the book before class. Call the bookstore at 362-2131 ext. 4022 before coming in.

2. Get extra help immediately if you feel you need it. I am available for extra help 24 hours a day 7 days a week except Sundays from midnight to 6 a.m. I need to sleep sometime. We will work in groups and I will try to arrange study groups outside of class. Tutors will be available also and the math lab is open many hours during the week on a walk in basis.

With all the help available you can't not pass.

3. Back to number 1. The most important thing for you to do is try as many problems before class as possible. That is correct! I am not delirious. But you say "How can I do the problems before they are explained to me?" That is the very essence of this course; to help you gain your math independence. We will work together in class on the material of the day. By the time the class is over you will know what you are doing.

You will need plenty of time for homework. If you have a job or family pressures you will need to schedule your hours to allow for blocks of time to study. Experience shows that you need at least 3 hours outside of class for each hour of class. Some people need lots more. I suggest you do about an hour at a time instead of trying to do all the work at once. When you are studying math you can only do so much before you need a break.

I am enclosing a copy of the schedule. Please review chapter 1. This is considered a review, material covered in basic math. I am also enclosing a writing assignment for you to complete before the first class. Bring it with you on Sept. 6. Your math autobiography will help me get to know you better. Please type it.

If you have any questions or concerns about doing algebra in the Fall please feel free to call me at home at 428-7538 or at school at 362-2131 x421. I have answering machines at both places so you can leave a message and I will return your call.

One last word; if you are concerned about anything I have written here, relax! There are many opportunities for extra help inside and outside of the class. If you are willing to work at it I can guarantee you will pass this course.

I look forward to seeing you on Sept. 6 to start a fun and interesting Fall semester.

Sincerely yours

Ted Panitz

P.S. If you have any comics or jokes about math or using math please bring them to class for extra credit.

WAC-WRITING ACTIVITY #1B

STUDENT AUTOBIOGRAPHY-WRITTEN PRIOR TO THE START OF THE COURSE

Description

Would you like to have your students reflect upon their role and/or interest in your class or upon their past educational history and experiences in your subject matter prior to attending the first class? Better yet, wouldn't it be outstanding if your students completed a writing assignment prior to the first class? These objectives and other benefits occur when students are asked to write their autobiographies either in conjunction with the professors letter to students prior to the semester or after the first class has been completed.

My students have a problem concerning my math classes which I would like us to start dealing with even before the semester begins. Their problem is math anxiety. How can I get them to address this problem without creating more anxiety? The approach I have taken is to ask them to write about how they feel about math and to describe their past experiences in math courses through the medium of an autobiography. Most students at the developmental math level and many others at the college math level have strong math anxieties. Perhaps many of us do also. The autobiography encourages students to reflect upon their reactions to previous math classes and to experiences they have had which may have created their math anxieties.

In addition to addressing specific questions the professor may have about his/her students there is a very subtle benefit associated with this exercise in that it draws out students who have an interest or ability to write but lack the expertise or confidence in the subject matter of the course. This is especially true in the field of mathematics, science and technology. Students often feel that they have abilities only in one area such as English. By associating writing with technical classes we begin, even if indirectly, to expand students awareness of their abilities in these areas.

An example of a success story regarding the benefit of writing in math involves an older, returning student who was majoring in English and took my beginning algebra course during a Fall semester. Her math anxiety level and lack of confidence was virtually paralyzing her on exams. She had written a five page autobiography prior to class in which she stressed her interest and ability in writing. I was convinced that through writing she could come to understand math. She used the writing assignments which followed to explore the origins of her math anxiety. I also encouraged her to write about her feelings during tests and to write out her solutions in English as well as using algebraic symbols. This did the trick. The writing helped reduce her math anxiety to the point where she began excelling on exams. She continued this approach through intermediate algebra and went on to obtain the highest test average in a college level statistics course. She also published a wonderful article in the college's writing magazine on the subject of why students should take algebra.

I have since used this approach with other students who are proficient in writing but math phobic with great success. The process starts with their completing their math autobiography.

Purposes and Benefits

1. The autobiographies provide valuable background information about students, including their past experiences and present concerns about the course.

2. The assignment communicates to students an interest in them as individuals versus their simply representing listening heads in a class.

3. Teachers can identify and deal with general concerns expressed by students or specific problems raised by individuals.

4. A basis for discussing general student concerns as a whole class exercise is provided. Students often feel alone in their anxieties. When they discuss their concerns in class they are usually comforted when they hear many other students expressing the same concerns.

5. The autobiographies cause students to reflect upon the class and previous experiences they have had with similar courses.

6. Students are encouraged to communicate with the teacher. Students may find it easier to write about their concerns rather than discuss them face to face with a professor with whom they are unfamiliar.

7. Writing as an integral part of the course is firmly established in the students minds. Writing in math classes is very unusual so students must be convinced of its value and appropriateness. Students generally feel good about being asked to write about themselves and expiring their math anxieties early in the class is cathartic.

8. The autobiography provides the teacher with a writing sample which helps identify the student's writing abilities.

9. The assignment establishes high expectations for the stu-

dents. The student will be expected to make a commitment to do extra work outside of the class.

10. It creates high expectations for the professor who illustrates how the course will have special elements to it which will make the course interesting and beneficial to the student.

Alternate Uses

1. A variety of questions may be posed in addition to general information. Student career goals, course goals, or reasons why students chose to attend an institution can be solicited.

2 The autobiography can be used to analyze student's writing ability.

3. The autobiography can be used to gage a students initial interest and commitment to the course based upon the detail and length of their work.

Implications/Applications for Collaborative Learning Opportunities

1. Students working in pairs interview each other based upon their autobiographies and then introduce their partner to the class, paying particular attention to the specific questions asked by the professor.

2. Working in pairs or larger groups students list their goals for the class or concerns, their career interests, or reasons for attending the school. Groups share their lists with the entire class.

3. A student worksheet is included below which is used during the first class to help students focus on specific questions and concerns they have as well as to help them identify interests they have which they might share with their partner. This worksheet encourages students to elaborate upon their autobiographies.

WRITING IN MATH– IS THIS FOR REAL????

This course will include writing assignments which are intended to help you understand how you are doing in the course and reacting to it. They will also help me to understand how you are doing in the course. This may be new to you so I would ask your patience and perhaps your indulgence.

To start I would like you to write your math autobiography using the following questions as a guideline. You do not have to answer them in order but please do include all the topics. Also write in narrative form, not single sentence responses. Please type using double spaces. I will collect them the first day and return them by the next class.

WHY ARE YOU TAKING THIS COURSE?

HAVE YOU TAKEN MATH AT 4C'S BEFORE, WHEN?

WHEN WAS THE LAST TIME YOU TOOK MATH? HOW DID YOU DO THEN? WHY?

HOW DO YOU FEEL ABOUT MATH? ANY IDEA WHY YOU FEEL THAT WAY?

(please be candid with this question, I am never offended by an honest answer)

WHAT IS YOUR MAJOR AND HOW WILL THIS COURSE FIT INTO IT?

WHAT TYPE OF EXPERIENCES HAVE YOU HAD IN MATH BEFORE?

WHAT WOULD YOU LIKE TO TELL ME ABOUT YOURSELF THAT I DIDN'T ASK?

The writing part of this course is very important and will be new to you in a math course. I take it very seriously and will collect the assignments and return them to you. They are not graded but help to provide a different way of communicating about the course and math.

The key to understanding math is reading and writing, not algebra or arithmetic. Thus I want us to work on writing as a means of reinforcing our reading applied to math.

<u>When you are finished add a headline to your autobiography as though it were a newspaper article. Use your imagination.</u>

IF YOU CAN EXPRESS YOURSELF IN WRITING THEN YOU UNDERSTAND WHAT YOU ARE DOING. A famous quote by author and scholar—Ted Panitz.

Student Sample Autobiography

STUDENT HOPES FOR MORE POSITIVE
MATH ATTITUDE

As a full time student at Cape Cod Community College, I have just completed my second semester. I'm taking this course during the Summer because I'm registered to take pre-calculus 1 in the Fall. As you know, Intermediate Algebra is a prerequisite for pre-calculus 1.

I took Elementary Algebra at Cape Cod Community College during the Fall semester, 1990. Prior to that, the last math course I took was in the Summer of 1968 at North Shore Community College. The only thing I remember about it was the fact that I passed the course.

Until a year ago I had a career in banking. I left banking to return to school. I'm working towards a degree in Accounting and plan to transfer to UMass, Boston, after I receive a degree from 4C's. Ultimately, my goal is to establish an accounting practice. Certainly math is more important to the major I've chosen.

I have no strong feelings one way or another towards math. I see math as a very dry subject and have a hard time getting excited about it. My experiences with math courses at 4C's have been limited. The Elementary Algebra course I took was taught by an instructor who knew the subject but didn't make the course interesting at all. I started Intermediate Algebra in the Spring semester 1991, but after two weeks of classes I dropped the course. I could tell that I didn't have the time to put into the course and still keep up with the other courses I was taking. Intermediate Algebra is the only course that I'. taking this Summer. I', prepared to put in the time needed to do well in the class.

The one thing I'd like you to know is that of the two sections offered this Summer for Intermediate Algebra, I signed up for this section because of the instructor. Last Summer I polled many students who were taking algebra (either Elementary or Intermediate) about their instructor. When I heard about Ted Panitz's method of teaching I was intrigued. I think that there's a good chance I may come away from this course with a more positive attitude towards math.

WAC - EXERCISE #1C

STUDENT PROFILE FOR FIRST CLASS INTRODUCTIONS

DESCRIPTION

The first class meeting of most courses consists of the professor going over the course syllabus, class procedures, and course policies. This is followed by the first content lecture. Some teachers ask students to fill our information sheets to obtain their class schedules and some autobiographical information such as employment, family backgrounds, majors etc. This material is reviewed by the instructor and rarely shared with the students. Students are often overwhelmed by the amount of material covered on the first day and probably retain very little.

This assignment is intended to be used with a different first class procedure. In cooperative learning classes warm-up activities designed to help students get to know each other often proceed class work. Students are asked to interview each other and report their findings to the whole class. In order to help students focus on questions of interest they are asked to write about themselves. In this case the affective nature of learning algebra is of interest to the professor who wishes the students to share their feelings about math which are usually negative.

This process helps students understand that they are not alone in their anxieties about math and often share common feelings and reactions to a difficult subject. By discussing their feeling amongst themselves and with the class their anxiety can be reduced substantially. A hidden advantage to this type of assignment is that it signals to the student that the instructor is aware of their feelings and is willing to discuss them openly and thus begin the process of dealing with classroom anxieties. Once students are comfortable talking to a new classmate they then may be asked to read the syllabus together and ask questions if they do not understand some aspect of the course. This is much more effective than having the professor tell the students what is in the syllabus.

The profiles may be collected by the professor after the group introductions are completed. This assignment combined with a student autobiography often provides a complete picture of each student and signals that the professor is interested in finding out as much about the student as they wish to communicate with the idea that this information will help the professor help the student. Students often add more information on their profiles than they have given in their autobiographies.

Purposes

1. To have students focus on and articulate answers to questions about themselves in preparation for interviewing their peers.

2. To provide autobiographical information about students in order to help the instructor gain a better understanding of his students and potential problems or pressures they are dealing with inside and outside of class.

3. To create a method of communication between students and between students and professors early in the semester.

4. To emphasize the importance of writing in the class using non-content based writing in class as well as outside of class.

5. To provide a mechanism to introduce the idea of using co-operative learning structures at the beginning of the course.

Alternate Uses

1. The profile question may be changed to fit specific needs or interests of different subject classes. For example: students might be asked about their interest in or travel to historic sites for a history focus.

2. Students might be asked to identify common interests, geographical residences, hobbies etc. with intent to help students find commonalties among themselves.

3. The profile and interview process may be used to help students form groups larger than pairs by helping them get to know class members. If self selection is allowed in the formation of groups then students will need to get to know their peers before making decisions about forming groups.

Implications/Applications for Collaborative Learning Opportunities:

1. This exercise is intended to be used as a stimulating activity to prepare students to share information using a cooperative structure called Pairs Interview. Students may refer to the forms during their interviews or write additional information on the reverse side of the form prior to introducing their partner to the whole class.

2. This activity provides an excellent mechanism for students to get to know other students in the class using an informal approach. Prior to introducing their partners to the whole class they might be asked to introduce each other in foursomes with the intent of beginning the process of creating larger groupings for future cooperative activities.

3. This activity might be repeated within groups over several classes in order to help students get to know as many classmates as possible in a short period of time. They would then be able to make well informed decisions about who they wished to work with when groups are formed for cooperative activities.

ALGEBRA- INTRODUCTION QUESTIONS

Name _____ Course/section_____

Major (If you have one) _____

Town Where you Live _____
Phone_____

HOW DO YOU FEEL ABOUT MATH AND WHY?
_____
_____
_____

WHAT IS YOUR BIGGEST CONCERN ABOUT THIS COURSE? EXPLAIN WHY?_____
_____
_____
_____

WHAT IS YOUR GOAL IN TAKING THIS COURSE?
(WHAT DO YOU HOPE TO ACCOMPLISH OR LEARN
DURING THE SEMESTER IN THIS COURSE)

_____

_____

_____

LIST YOUR HOBBIES, SPECIAL INTERESTS, TRAVELS,
OTHER INFORMATION WHICH WILL HELP ME GET
TO KNOW YOU BETTER.

_____

_____

_____

Student Responses

HOW DO YOU FEEL ABOUT MATH AND WHY?

1. I Hate it. I have a horrible time following it. I have always struggled.

2. I like algebra and I enjoy the challenge, but I do not care much for the more intense courses.

3. I don't think of it as one of my strengths. I don't find math very exciting or interesting.

4. It's not my greatest subject. It's always been an obstacle or so I perceive it to be.

5. Math gives me an instant headache because I haven't gotten to a point of understanding it.

6. Angst!! It doesn't come easy to.

7. After taking the course last semester I don't hate math, but I know my strengths and weaknesses.

WHAT IS YOUR BIGGEST CONCERN ABOUT THIS COURSE? EXPLAIN WHY?

1. My main concern is that I will not understand it from day one.

2. I do not have any concerns about the class because I like math and plan on studying hard.

3 That I will fall behind and not understand what is being taught.

4. That I will lose interest and my work will suffer. That is what happened the last time I took this class in high school.

5. That since we only meet once a week I won't get the 1:1 I need to pass.

6. Passing–I never took it before and feel it may be difficult.

7. To understand the material I didn't last time around, that I might not comprehend it.

WHAT IS YOUR GOAL IN TAKING THIS COURSE? (WHAT DO YOU HOPE TO ACCOMPLISH OR LEARN DURING THE SEMESTER IN THIS COURSE?)

1. I hope to pass and satisfy a math prerequisite for a college math course.

2. I hope to learn new equations for use in my job.

3. I want to pass this course so I can move on to a harder course next semester.

4. I hope to finally learn how to master the problems.

5. The basics of math, obviously, and I'd like to view myself as more than adequate in the subject.

6. My goal is to pass and move along to Algebra II and to learn that my worries were for nothing.

7. To pass with flying colors!

LIST YOUR HOBBIES, SPECIAL INTERESTS, TRAVELS, OTHER INFORMATION WHICH WILL HELP ME GET TO KNOW YOU BETTER.

ANALYZING THE SEVEN PRINCIPLES OF GOOD EDUCATION

Description

On the first day of classes students usually follow a procedure where they show up in class, receive a course syllabus and hear an explanation about course policies, assignments and procedures. From then on they simply come to class, listen to a lecture and leave with a ream of lecture notes. They expect the professor to tell them everything they need to know to complete the course. Students are rarely asked to reflect upon the nature of good learning and their roles in the process. Students are even less frequently asked to make suggestions about class procedures or alternative approaches which might help them learn more effectively.

Imagine the surprise students receive when after three or four classes they are asked to review and write an analysis of the Seven Principles Of Good Education and think of ways to apply the principles in their class. Consider the positive impact created when their ideas are actually adopted. This exercise sends a clear message to students that you want them involved in their education and not just acting as passive recipients of information.

Courses which use collaborative learning and interactive techniques rely heavily on student participation in groups, as part of whole class discussions, and student demonstrations of their work. Students need to be convinced that this approach is beneficial and helpful to their learning. By using the Seven Principles student attention can be focused upon the need for active and collaborative learning as well as ideas such as time on task needed to succeed in the course and the benefit of an interactive relationship between professor and student. The purpose of using the Wingspread Journal article is to present the material from the perspective of an "outside" expert. Having students analyze the principles and relate them to their own experiences and the class helps them internalize the concepts which will lead to their success in the class.

Finally, if a professor is using collaborative learning techniques then it becomes important to model the process of participation and sharing the power associated with organizing and running a course. This can be accomplished by discussing suggestions made by students and encouraging the class to help decide which suggestions are appropriate for use during the class. For professors who do not use collaborative learning techniques this exercise is also helpful since the seven principles are inclusive of many concepts necessary for good education in addition to interactive learning modes.

Purposes

1. To highlight important factors which lead to a good learning environment and student success.

2. To involve students in evaluating the components of good education.

3. To include students in structuring course procedures through their suggestions on how to apply the seven principles to their classes.

4. The assignment focuses the students attention on the value of certain class procedures and activities such as collaborative and active learning techniques.

5. The professor may use this article to emphasize the need for sufficient time on task to insure student success in the course.

6. The information about success strategies when presented from the perspective of an expert may have an additional impact upon the students attitude about learning.

7. This exercise communicates the professors values and approaches to providing the best educational experience possible.

8. When this assignment is given after the completion of 3 or 4 classes it gives the students an opportunity to compare what is happening in class with the seven principles, thus reinforcing the appropriate nature of the instructional procedure. This is especially helpful when collaborative learning the paradigm used.

9. Students have an opportunity to write to the professor to express concerns they have or make suggestions about particular class procedures which they might not feel comfortable doing verbally.

Alternate Uses:

1. Individual items within the seven principles may be analyzed more extensively in order to help students to understand why certain class procedures are used.

2. Students may be asked to relate the seven principles to their real life situations in order to help them see how they apply outside of a class environment.

3. In a similar vein, students may be asked to relate the seven principles to course content and then course content to real life situations. For older students this internalizing effect of their education is especially important.

4. This activity may be used as a graded writing assignment in English, education, or social science classes etc.

Implication/Applications for Collaborative Learning Opportunities:

1. Think-pair-share can be used to involve pairs of students in analyzing the seven principles. Students write out their assessment of the seven principles, share their observations with a partner and then report their results to the whole class.

2. Working in groups of 3-4 students are asked to prioritize the list according to which items they feel have the strongest impact on learning. Other criteria can be used, such as which items are most likely to be accepted by students or which items are most feasible.

3. Group brainstorming techniques can be introduced to identify additional ideas which promote good education, followed by a presentation of these ideas to the whole class.

4. Working in pairs or larger groups students develop ways in which the seven principles can be applied in class.

5. Working collaboratively students identify how the seven principles may be applied in their everyday lives including employment, home, and social environments.

ALGEBRA WRITING ASSIGNMENT

I WOULD LIKE YOU TO ANALYZE THE ATTACHED LIST OF PRINCIPLES SUGGESTED FOR GOOD UNDER-GRADUATE EDUCATION. IN PARTICULAR PLEASE AN-SWER THE FOLLOWING QUESTIONS AND ADD ANY AD-DITIONAL OBSERVATIONS OR COMMENTS YOU WOULD LIKE TO.

-HOW DO THESE PRINCIPLES APPLY TO ALGEBRA?

-CAN YOU THINK OF ACTIVITIES THAT WOULD BE HELPFUL IN OUR CLASS WHICH WOULD FACILITATE THE PRINCIPLES?

-DOES THE IDEA OF WORKING WITH OTHER PEOPLE CONCERN YOU?

-PLEASE ADD ANY ADDITIONAL COMMENTS YOU FEEL ARE APPROPRIATE TO THIS TOPIC OR FOR RUNNING THE CLASS.

PLEASE SUBMIT AS A MINIMUM A ONE PAGE TYPED ANALYSIS. ALSO IT WOULD BE HELPFUL TO ME IF YOU ADDRESSED EACH OF THE SEVEN PRINCIPLES, IN WHAT EVER ORDER YOU FEEL COMFORTABLE WITH. I AM VERY INTERESTED IN HEARING YOUR THOUGHTS ON THIS ARTICLE SINCE MY PHILOSOPHY OF TEACHING AND EDUCATION, IF NOT LIFE, IS EMBODIED IN THESE IDEAS. IT WILL BE ESPECIALLY HELPFUL TO ME TO GET YOUR INPUT, SUGGESTIONS, AND HEAR YOUR CONCERNS AT THIS EARLY STAGE OF THE SEMESTER. YOU MAY WRITE WHAT EVER YOU THINK. I AM NEVER OFFENDED BY CONSTRUCTIVE CRITICISM OR OBSERVATIONS.

SEVEN PRINCIPLES FOR GOOD PRACTICE IN UNDERGRADUATE EDUCATION

by Arthur W. Chickering and Zelda F. Gamson
From the Wingspread Journal— special edition

Summary

Following is a brief summary of the Seven Principles for Good Practice in Undergraduate Education as compiled in a study supported by the American Association of Higher Education, the Education Commission of States, and the Johnson Foundation.

1. GOOD PRACTICE ENCOURAGES STUDENT FACULTY CONTACT

Frequent student-faculty contact in and out of classes is the most important factor in student motivation and involvement. Faculty concern helps students get through rough times and keep on working. Knowing a few faculty members well enhances students' intellectual commitment and encourages them to think about their own values and future plans.

2. GOOD PRACTICE ENCOURAGES COOPERATION AMONG STUDENTS

Learning is enhanced when it is more like a team effort than a solo race. Good learning, like good work, is collaborative and social, not competitive and isolated. Working with others often increases involvement in learning. Sharing one's own ideas and responding to others' reactions improves thinking and deepens understanding.

3. GOOD PRACTICE ENCOURAGES ACTIVE LEARNING

Learning is not a spectator sport. Students do not learn much just sitting in classes listening to teachers, memorizing pre-packaged assignments and spitting out answers. They must talk about what they are learning, write about it, relate it to past experiences, and apply it to their daily lives. They must make what they learn part of themselves.

4. GOOD PRACTICE GIVES PROMPT FEEDBACK

Knowing what you know and don't know focuses learning.

Students need appropriate feedback on performance to benefit from courses. In getting started, students need help in assessing existing knowledge and competence. In classes, students need frequent opportunities to perform and receive suggestions for improvement. At various points during college, and at the end, students need chances to reflect on what they have learned, what they still need to know, and how to assess themselves.

5. GOOD PRACTICE EMPHASIZES TIME ON TASK

Time plus energy equals learning. There is no substitute for time on task. Learning to use one's time well is critical for students and professional alike. Students need help in learning effective time management. Allocating realistic amounts of time means effective learning for students and effective teaching for faculty. How an institution defines time expectations for students, faculty and administrators, and other professional staff can establish the basis for high performance for all.

6. GOOD PRACTICE COMMUNICATES HIGH EXPECTATIONS

Expect more and you will get it. High expectations are important for everyone–for the poorly prepared, for those unwilling to exert themselves, and for the bright and well motivated. Expecting students to perform well becomes a self-fulfilling prophecy when teachers and institutions hold high expectations of themselves and make extra efforts.

7. GOOD PRACTICE RESPECTS DIVERSE TALENTS AND WAYS OF LEARNING

There are many roads to learning. people bring different talents and styles of learning to college. Brilliant students in the seminar room may be all thumbs in the lab or art studio. Students rich in hands-on experience may not do so well in theory. Students need to opportunity to show their talents and learn in ways that work for them. Then they can be pushed to learning in new ways that do not come so easily.

STUDENT RESPONSES

I think the article on the Seven Principles for Good Practice in Undergraduate Education are concepts all schools should adopt, whether colleges, high schools or elementary schools. I have found for myself that communicating with instructors who make themselves accessible gives me a morale boost, as they have worked with me when I have had personal problems which interfered with my class work. Having the lines of communication open gives my instructors reasons when I am absent from class or why I did not do as well on an exam as I should have. Instructors I have had have been very understanding and helpful. This makes it so I do not feel as guilty and gives me encouragement to achieve more because they have been understanding. I do not constantly have things happen, but with raising three children on my own, from time to time something does arise which I have no control over, and they still take priority over my own studies.

When it comes to team effort I agree. I personally do not like to feel I am competing for top grades with other students. I do find working with others gives me a better feeling about myself and those around me. I like to hear others' ideas and thoughts. Sometimes it has changed my own view of the situation. I have to agree also with the statement that students do not learn much from listening to lectures and taking notes. Working in groups as we have been doing in this class, helps to relax the atmosphere and reduce anxiety. Having someone to work with on a problem helps both of us to understand it. Then sometimes we can say "ah, we aren't so dumb!." It helps in algebra to do the problems on the board, and also to do the worksheets in class. Also to be able to say "Well this is how I was taught to do this," and then to learn there is a way to do the problem that is easier.

I think in your class you are already bringing out the seven items. So far I have not felt the anxiety I usually feel in math class, making it easier for me to learn. The idea of working together with other people does not really concern me unless I am working with a student who really just does not care or if the person gives the sigh of superiority when I do not understand something. Otherwise I have no complaint.

In a symphony orchestra, there is a large group of people and a conductor who leads many different kinds of people, playing a wide variety of musical instruments. There are the strings, brass, woodwind and percussion sections needed to present the beautiful sound of music. Its a blending of individuality by homogeneous elements. Like a great conductor, a teacher is one who leads or shows the right way for his/her students in their learning and understanding new material. Teachers ask for feedback from their students, so that he/she may be able to be assisted in their learning process. Not everyone is in tune with each other all the time, while they are learning something new. It takes a good teacher to help motivate and build one's own expectations.

Students are all different, no two are the same; each one has his/her own past experiences in learning, some were good, some were not. It's nice having a teacher walk into the classroom with a smile on their face. It makes everyone feel comfortable, instead of feeling as though they are about to be blindfolded and placed in front of a firing squad, to face the task of algebra. It's not just a learning experience, it's an improvement towards our future goals. I like working in groups, learning different ways of doing math. I have never been taught math in this manner before. Some ideas from the other students have helped me get a better grasp on algebra. I look forward to the rest of the semester.

WAC - EXERCISE #1E

STUDENT/PROFESSOR SUCCESS CONTRACT

Description

A contract entered into by two parties is legally binding on both signatories. When we buy a house we sign a mortgage contract and fully intend to live up to its terms by making monthly payments, real estate payments and purchasing home owners insurance. Contracts for other services are equally important parts of our lives. Why not ask our students to enter into a learning contract with us since both students and professors have a vested interest in the outcome?

This exercise is designed with two goals in mind. The first is to highlight the approaches and responsibilities undertaken by the professor and the second is to emphasize student's responsibilities along with suggested activities which will help them succeed in the course. The use of a contract helps formalize the suggestions and putting them into a legal framework underlines the serious nature of the items agreed to by the students and the professor.

When offered the success contract, students are initially taken aback by its legal structure, then they become amused by the thought of this approach to encouraging their learning, and finally they express appreciation at my effort to outline exactly what I am prepared to do on their behalf in exchange for their commitment to work hard in the class. For students who doubt the seriousness of this exercise I often bring a copy of the contract to class to review the items which I feel students may be letting down on. Students will remind me of my part of the agreement if they feel I have forgotten to carry out some aspect of the contract.

This exercise helps focus on student study habits and approaches which are critical to the success of the course. It reaffirms the collaborative nature of the class and the fact that student participation is encouraged in a non-threatening, risk free environment. As with all writing assignments this activity opens a line of communication between student and professor which would not otherwise be available.

Purposes

1. To highlight the importance of the responsibilities of the student and professor which will help both succeed in meeting the course objectives.

2. To call the students attention to and emphasize the type of study habits needed for this course and the time required to complete homework assignments etc.

3. To encourage students to seek help early in the semester if the need arises. This is especially important in math courses where students can fall behind, never to catch up.

4. To identify a variety of sources of help available to students and encourage their use.

5. To emphasize the professors concern for his/her students success in the course.

6. To demonstrate the value of writing in class and provide an example of the professors writing style.

---

7. To provide an alternate form of communication between the professor and students.

Alternate Uses

1. The contract may be altered to encourage students to commit to meeting specific course objectives such as writing five essays, or one term paper, or completing three exams and a final exam, etc.

2. Students may be asked to write their own contract specifying activities they will pursue in order to meet the course objectives.

3. Additional items may be added according to special circumstances provided in different classes.

Implications/Application for Collaborative Learning Opportunities

1. Pairs read the entire contract and alternating between each one explains an item and the other verifies the explanation.

2. Groups brainstorm how they intend to implement the contract.

3. Groups develop their own contracts to meet the course objectives or their personal objective.

4. Groups edit or rewrite the existing contract.

ALGEBRA SUCCESS CONTRACT

THIS CONTRACT SHALL BE ENTERED INTO BE-
TWEEN THE COURSE INSTRUCTOR, TED PANITZ AND
_____, IN ORDER TO GUARANTEE
SUCCESS IN ALGEBRA. EACH SIGNATORY TO THIS
AGREEMENT AGREES TO THE FOLLOWING ITEMS LISTED
BELOW AS EVIDENCED BY THEIR SIGNATURES.

I, Ted Panitz, as the instructor of algebra agree to the following actions to be taken by me to insure your success in this course.

- I will provide answers to your questions in a variety of ways
which will include your participation.
- I will make the class fun and interesting.
- I will solicit your comments on class activities and your reactions to my methods and try to adapt your suggestions to class
procedures.
- I will explain my rationale behind the activities I use in class.
- I will not take personally any comments you make in class that
are made in the spirit of participation and constructive criticism intended to help us succeed.
- I will never criticize or belittle anyone for asking a question or
raising a classroom issue.
- I will do everything I can to help you succeed in this course
providing you have met your half of the contract.
- I will encourage new ideas for approaching the study of math
and to try to include them in class.

_____
Signed

I _____ HEREBY AGREE TO THE FOLLOWING ACTIONS TO BE TAKEN ON MY PART TO INSURE MY SUCCESS IN ALGEBRA.

- I will commit myself to spend one hour minimum on each section assigned.
- I will read the section assigned before the class and attempt to do the problems at the end of the section. I will check the answers to all the work I attempt.
- If I cannot get the correct answer to a problem I will not get mad or give up. I will put the problem number on the board at the next class, and continue working on the rest of the section problems.
- I will take the chapter review and correct it before doing the chapter mastery demonstration in class.
- I will work with other people in class in groups of varying size.
- I will try to help other students as well as ask for help if I need it.
- If I have a problem I cannot solve I will share it with the class verbally or by putting it on the board for all of us to work on and discuss.
- I will seek extra help outside of class, early in the semester, if I feel I need it, from Ted, in the math lab, or in the Academic Development Center.
- If I cannot complete the class because of personal reasons or health problems I will not simply leave without first discussing alternatives with Ted. please add your comments, suggestions or contract items on the reverse side.

_____

Signed   date

STUDENT RESPONSES

The idea of signing a contract initially startled me until I read what you said you would do for us and then after I read what you asked me to do. This makes a lot of sense in this algebra class. It takes a lot of time to be good at math and I need to reminded about that.

I like the idea of your telling us what you will do to help us in the class and I will definitely take you up on your offer for extra help. You will be seeing a lot of me this semester.

This is the first time I have had a teacher ask me to sign any kind of contract at all. I think it tells me that you really want us to get through this class and do well and will work as hard as you want us to work. The offer for extra help is very reassuring and I like the suggestions about going to the math lab. Last semester in basic math I waited for several weeks before trying the math lab since I had never been there before. I wish I had been encouraged to go there sooner. I am not too sure about the idea of working with other students in groups but I am willing to give it a try, especially since you think it will be helpful to us. Working in groups so far has been fun and it has helped me learn the rules better as long as I know that I don't have to learn everything on my own and the teacher will be there to help us if we need it.

Wow! Next you will be asking us to sign over our car titles or first born children. I looked for the fine print and couldn't find any so I conclude that what you see is what you get. I like what I see! Giving me a list of what you are going to do for us was very reassuring and a little unconventional. I expected the professor to tell us what was expected of us and not the other way around. This seems consistent with they way you are running the class. We have only had a few classes but I can see already that this will be a different math class than I have ever had before. For one thing I have not been asked to do any writing in math classes before and this is the fourth piece of writing to come my way in just two weeks (your letter, my autobiography, the seven principles and now this contract). I am beginning to appreciate your strategy more. Some students are grumbling about writing in math but I think it is a great idea. I see myself more as an English person so writing is fun for me where the math is not (sorry, but you wanted us to be honest). I will try my best to meet the items on the contract which I have signed and I can see that you are already meeting most of the ones you have signed off on. By the way, what is the penalty if we break the contract? Just kidding of course!

Suggestions for additional contract items:

The following sugestions are typical responses students have when asked for additional items for the contract. This is where student concerns will surface as part of this writing exercise, especially for those students who are not familiar with collaborative learning techniques,

For Ted:
- Offer study/review sessions out of class.
- Review material in class prior to exams.
- Lecture more on new material.
- Work more problems on the board.
- Answer questions more directly.

For Students:
- Form study groups with at least two other students outside of class.
- Exchange phone numbers with at least five other students.
- Make up material missed from class due to absences.
- Call Ted at home or at school if you are stuck on a problem before quitting.

2-PERSONAL REFLECTION/ MOTIVATION

Most college classes are run linearly. Information is presented by the instructor based upon the course syllabus and schedule. An exam or other assessment is given to verify that students have obtained and retained the course content and then the process is repeated using new content material. There is little time or effort made to have students reflect upon their performance or class procedures. The writing assignments presented in this section direct students to assess themselves at various points in the semester and create opportunities for them to affect the direction or procedures used in the class. Students are asked to reflect on their performance after the first exam and make suggestions for their improvement and how the professor might assist them. A mid semester review and mid semester push may be used to help students stay focused on the tasks facing them as they move through the semester and try to deal with many pressures placed upon them by academic and outside social demands. Finally an end of semester self evaluation asks students to reflect upon their performance and structure of the course. Professors may obtain valuable insights into their teaching methods depending upon which questions they ask students as part of the evaluation. This can also be also be accomplished by asking students to write a letter to a friend describing the course and how they felt they performed in the class.

A- Student post exam questionnaire
B- Students write a letter to a friend–an unusual course evaluation
C- Mid semester course review & student evaluation
D- Mid semester push–or how do I survive all my professors' demands

---

E- Final semester push
F- End of semester student self-evaluation

WAC - EXERCISE #2A

STUDENT POST EXAM QUESTIONNAIRE

DESCRIPTION

What is wrong with the following scenario regarding test taking in college courses? Students appear for the exam, complete the exam, hand it in and leave the room, receive their graded results within a few classes and then proceed to work toward the next exam as the process repeats itself over and over during the semester. Some professors will discuss the exam results in terms of the class average and standard deviation or what areas were especially poorly done, but rarely do students reflect upon their performance or consider ways of improving. There is little effort made to improve preparation for exams by the students or to review the evaluation process designed by the professor.

The student post exam questionnaire breaks the cycle by asking students to reflect upon their responses and feelings regarding their performance on the first semester exam. A mastery approach is used in my courses. Students are given an opportunity to correct mistakes immediately upon completion of the exam. This exercise asks students to articulate and write about their feelings after completing the exam, after they have made their corrections, and when they receive their exam back with the final grade. They are also asked to consider what they need to do to improve their performance and what I can do to help them. The exercise is started in class immediately after the exams are returned in order to get the student's initial reactions to the test and their score. The questions regarding what they and I can do to improve are completed as a homework assignment to allow more time for thoughtful consideration. I return each of the student questionnaires with my comments and suggestions at the next class.

There is a certain surprise element to this exercise because students have not previously been asked to think about their performance and reactions to exams and they have certainly not been asked to make recommendations about the format of the course or exam. The exercise calls attention to my interest in their learning how to learn in addition to learning the course content. Perhaps as significant, it provides an additional mechanism for communication between students and professors about each others performance.

Purposes:

1. Provide a mechanism for communication between students and the professor.

2. To extend the evaluation process, which is inherent in examinations, beyond the course content to the students' approach to testing.

3. To encourage students to reconsider their study habits and methods.

4. To focus students' attention on their reactions to the exam and their performance on the exam and to communicate their observations to the professor.

5. To emphasize the professors desire to help them prepare for exams which evaluate their performance in the course.

6. To actively seek ways of improving the exam structure in order to insure consistency in course objectives and examinations.

7. To make the course interactive and thus be consistent with the paradigm of collaborative learning.

8. To encourage students to take responsibility for their learning.

9. To involve the students in the development of the course by soliciting their suggestions about the exam structure, perhaps for inclusion in future courses.

Alternate Uses

1. Students may be asked to do a form of item analysis to identify levels of difficulty of each question.

2. Different questions may be asked according to the interests of different professors.

3. Students could be asked to write about their study habits

---

and approach to exam preparation in addition to their reactions and feelings.

Implications/Applications for collaborative Learning Opportunities

1. Students working in pairs discuss their performance on and reaction to the exam and report back to the class (this part may be made optional).

2. Students working in groups of three or more to develop a list of actions which could use to improve their understanding of the material and their performance on the exam.

3. In a similar vein groups brainstorm different in-class or out-of-class activities which would help improve their understanding of the material and test performance.

4. This exercise may be used to establish study groups or out-of-class support groups among students.

5. Students work in groups to develop problems for future exams.

INTERMEDIATE ALGEBRA SURVEY FOLLOWING THE FIRST TEST

NAME_____

I would like you to answer the following questions regarding your reaction to the first test. Please feel free to make any observations or comments you feel would help me to understand how you performed and reacted to the first test situation and to help you focus on a strategy for improving on future tests. Use the reverse side if you need more room to write.

1) How did you feel after you finished the test on the first day?

_____

_____

_____

2) How did you feel after the second attempt at the test and making corrections?

_____

_____

_____

3) How did you feel when you received the test back and
saw your grade?

_____

_____

4) What can you do to improve your performance if you
think it needs it and what can I do to facilitate your test taking?

_____

_____

_____

STUDENT RESPONSE

INTERMEDIATE ALGEBRA SURVEY
FOLLOWING THE FIRST TEST

NAME   STUDENT X

1) How did you feel after you finished the test on the first
day?

> I needed more time and wished I had reviewed for my-
> self some things that were on the test that we did not go over
> in class, e.g. polynomial division. I had to review it during
> the test, which took up time.

2) How did you feel after the second attempt at the test and
making corrections?

> Good. Fairly confident. Actually I rather enjoy trying
> to figure out where I went wrong, although I wouldn't make
> silly mistakes just for the pleasure. Frankly, because I hadn't
> reviewed enough on my own, I was still too rusty to deal with
> the time pressure without making mistakes.

3) How did you feel when you received the test back and saw
your grade?

> WONDERFUL! Especially when others who had both
> taken more and less time than I, with the same opportunity to
> make corrections, had not done as well. I was fortunate enough

_____

A Sourcebook of Ideas and Writing Exercises   35 not to have a class afterward so I could stay and finish up. But others that could have stayed did not. Obviously I am still very conscious of the length of time work takes me even at my best.

4) What can you do to improve your performance if you think it needs it and what can I do to facilitate your test taking?

I skimped on personal review time and felt a rusty discomfort during the test as a result. I managed however, because of the time I invested last semester. Suggestion for the review portion of the course. Remind the class of the cumulative review tests in the book as a means of doing self-review. I was unsure of where to focus my time and made the mistake of going through each chapter page by page. I didn't get very far. The cumulative review catches it all up and gets one accustomed to having the problem types mixed up. That mixture can temporarily throw off mental "cues" formed through the progressive pattern of the initial learning. If I had remembered the cumulative review tests in time they would have been helpful, but I simply forgot they were there.

WAC - EXERCISE #2B

Students write a letter to a friend - an unusual course evaluation

Description

Typical course/faculty evaluations use a Likert scale check off system with five categories ranging from 1= very poor to 5= excellent. A list of questions is provided and at the end of the form there may be space allotted for comments. Student signatures may be optional in some cases. The evaluations are usually completed by the students prior to the end of the semester before they have time to consider all aspects of the class. The types of questions posed are often vague, such as, "Did the instructor meet the course objectives?" or "Did the supplemental materials contribute to the course?" This approach is highly restrictive of thoughtful and constructive student input into improving the course through the use of an evaluation process.

This exercise approaches course evaluations from a completely different perspective, that of the students' perception of what occurred during the course, how they reacted to course procedures, and what actions they would recommend for other students to take to prepare for the class. Students are asked to describe the teaching style of the professor and how they felt about this approach as well as what they would differently if they were starting the course over again. The assignment statement can easily be modified to address specific questions or concerns the professor has and is open ended enough to allow students to add any comments they feel appropriate.

I use this exercise at the end of the semester to assess my teaching approach, which is based upon collaborative learning, by asking the students to explain how they view the course in retrospect. From the responses shown below I think you will see that the collaborative process has a very positive effect on the students and leaves them with a sound understanding of the material, a stronger self esteem and appreciation of this style of teaching. The testimonials provided before these are unedited and some contain constructive criticisms or comments that reflect some students difficulties in dealing with group learning.

Purposes

1. To provide a student centered mechanism for evaluating a course.

2. To enable and encourage students to give feedback on the course in a personal and extended manner. There is no limit set on the length of the letter.

3. To cause the students to reflect on the course, their reactions to working in a collaborative environment and their overall performance in the class.

4. To have students consider what improvements they might make in their study habits etc., in future courses, based upon their evaluation of their performance in this class.

5. To continue to use writing as a method of communication between the student and professor, which has been used throughout the semester.

6. To provide a course description for future classes.

7. To provide encouragement and assistance to students who will follow in the course.

Alternate Uses

1. This exercise need not be limited to the end of the semester but may be used at any time during the term in order to obtain student input into the teaching process or course structure.

2. Questions may be used to address student concerns, which were raised in other writing assignments, to see if improvements made are having the expected impact upon the students.

3. This exercise could be used as a graded essay in a writing course.

4. Students might be asked to write a letter about some aspect of the course content, such as putting themselves into a historical context, writing about a scientific finding or discovery, or writing about a social issue facing society, etc.

Implications/Applications for Collaborative Learning Opportunities

1. Students working in pairs write a letter based upon the same questions asked of individual students.

2. Students working in pairs write a letter to the professor, instead of to a friend, which critiques the class.

3. Pairs combine into groups of four and review and discuss each pair's letter to a friend or the professor.

4. Students write letters individually and then working together, using the process of peer review and editing, combine both exercises into one letter.

5. Students working in groups of 3-4 brainstorm suggestions for future students who will take the class, based upon their individual suggestions for new students. Combine all the groups suggestions into a master list of helpful hints for new students.

6. Students complete the above exercise with the focus being constructive suggestions for the professor.

ALGEBRA WRITING ASSIGNMENT-WRITE A LETTER TO A FRIEND

You know someone who is planning to take this course with Ted next semester. They have asked you to give them some advice and information about the course so they will have a better chance to succeed in the class. Among other things they would like to know what the course covers, what the style of the instructor is and how you handled the course including your approach to studying and participation in class. They have heard that the professor uses collaborative learning techniques in the class and would like you to explain what that entails.

What would you suggest people do to get ready for the class? Also, what things did you especially like and dislike about the course? What would you do differently if you had to do it over again? What would you advise they do to be sure to complete the course successfully?

You may add anything else that comes to your mind or subtract anything that does not. (Pardon the math humor but it was my last chance).

Student responses:

Dear friend,

Well, my algebra course with Ted Panitz is almost over, and I must say it has been much better than I expected. You know how frightened I was–I've always had a low opinion of my math abilities–bit Ted has made it almost impossible to fail this class.

First of all, Ted asked us to sign a contract guaranteeing that we would pass the course if we lived up to our part of the bargain. Our part of the agreement amounted to working very hard on homework assignments and participating in the classroom. For his part Ted has worked very hard at teaching, making the class interesting and giving feedback all along the way so that we always had a clear sense of how we were doing. I appreciate the fact that he is one of those teachers who is concerned more with his students learning the concepts of algebra rather than having them memorize theorems and equations. I really think that this is the class for you, if you need to take algebra.

Although I never thought I would be able to work with letters in place of numbers, I found that certain parts of the course were actually fun, partly because I gave it my best shot. There a few bits of advice I would give you. The first is don't fall behind on the homework! It is pretty important to go over the assigned modules in the textbook before Ted goes over them in class. Other advice came from Ted himself:

a) Don't think too hard about what you are doing- Some of this stuff works but is hard to rationalize, like negative numbers. Ted likes the commercial that says "Just Do It!"

b) Don't work on algebra for more than about an hour at a time.

c) The best way to prepare for a chess match is to be in top physical condition so that your mind functions clearly. A test is like a chess match. I personalized this chance bit of information and tried to exercise regularly, eat healthy meals, and get plenty of sleep. I think is helped me with my algebra.

I hope you will enjoy this class as much as I did. Although it wasn't my favorite subject, I fared much better than I expected. Ted has made it as painless as algebra could possibly be.

Educationally yours,

Dear friend,

This is my advice to you if you are planning to take elementary algebra with Ted Panitz. Relax, have a positive attitude, realize that you will succeed in the course, and enjoy the class. Also, in order to succeed in the course you must do the homework. If you don't do the homework, it may appear to be difficult and you may not feel confident about it.

The course covers most of the material in chapters 1-8 of the book as well as written assignments designed to help students understand the roll of mathematics in our daily lives. The style of the instructor is an effective one because he makes learning algebra fun and not frightening. He shows respect for the student as well as confidence in the fact the he or she will succeed. He initiates the student to participate in class with the use of groups. This helps the student to understand the material and relax while learning it.

I feel that I handled the class well because I approached it with an open mind and with confidence. I did the homework and participated in small groups. In order to get ready for the class I suggest that you chose to dismiss any further feeling of anxiety about math. If the subject intimidates you as it usually does me, continue a positive attitude throughout the course and dedicate yourself to the homework to the best of your ability.

What I liked about the course was the relaxed environment in which we learned and the teaching style of Ted Panitz. If I had to do it over again I would have asked for more instruction from the teacher in the areas where I had difficulty. In those areas where I did have difficulty, it was because I didn't do the homework completely because I had a busy week and didn't manage my time properly. So I advise you, when you take the course, be sure to complete all homework assignments so that you will feel confident and succeed. I enjoyed the class very much and recommend taking a math course with Ted Panitz.

WAC - EXERCISE #2C

MID SEMESTER COURSE REVIEW/STUDENT SELF EVALUATION

Description

Test scores on exams are one mechanism to determine how well students understand the content of a course but they fail to provide information on how students perceive they are progressing in and understanding the course concepts, whether any prob-

---

lems are developing for the students with the class, or whether there are other outside factors which might influence their future performance. As stated in WAC exercise #4, a problem with typical testing systems, used to evaluate student performance, is that exams do not encourage students to reflect upon non-content course areas such as study habits, their overall performance and confidence with the material, their relation to the professor and interactions with their peers. A high exam score encourages students to continue their efforts and low exam scores often discourage students without providing a mechanism for improvement.

The Mid Semester Course Review/Student Self Evaluation addresses this problem by asking students to identify factors in their lives which are impacting their performance in the class and equally importantly asks them to think of ways in which they can change their approach to address any factors which are having an adverse impact. There is inherent call for a commitment by students to make changes while they still have time to effect the outcome of the course. This exercise underscores the professors commitment to working with the students to help insure their success in the class.

When combined with collaborative learning activities and whole class discussions around this topic the activity becomes a powerful motivating force for individual students, groups working collaboratively and the professor. Students who enjoy writing especially enjoy this exercise since it allows them to express themselves using a medium they are comfortable with. In mathematics courses, where there can be a high level of student anxiety, this is especially helpful to the students and the professor.

Purposes

1. To have create a mechanism for students to review their progress and performance in the course midway through the term.

2. To encourage students to identify any problems areas which may be developing in the course and make changes if necessary while there is still time left in the term to effect the outcome.

3. To encourage students to understand and reinforce the good aspects of their performance.

4. To obtain input from students on the progress, structure and activities used to date in the course.

5. To provide a mechanism for students to communicate with the professor any personal problems or concerns they may have related to the class or to allow for positive observations by the students.

6. To provide a mechanism for the professor to communicate back to the students in writing or verbally.

Alternate Uses

1. Students report on their progress on a project, group activity, research project, or other course assignment.

2. Students produce a suggested work/study schedule for the remainder of the term.

3. Use the evaluations as a basis for professor/student conferences.

4. Use the evaluations to aid in student advising, pre-registration etc.

5. Use the student suggestions and class observations to incorporate changes in future classes.

Implications/Applications for Collaborative Learning Opportunities

1. Students working in pairs share their midterm evaluations and discuss problems they are having and possible solutions.

2. Using a whole class discussion develop a list of potential problems facing students and a second list of solutions.

3. Working in groups students develop a list of positive aspects of the class and areas for student improvement.

4. Using the information developed in part two the class as a whole develops a list of positive aspects of the class and areas for improvement.

5. Groups brainstorm ideas about how the professor might alter the course to help students improve their performance.

MID SEMESTER STUDENT SELF/ COURSE EVALUATION

We have reached the mid semester point in the term and have completed a number of exams and assignments. This information has provided you and I with helpful information about your understanding of the course content. There is still plenty of time remaining in the semester to make changes to your approach to the course and how I run the class. In order to take full advantage of this time and to have us both reflect on and evaluate our progress to date I would like you to think about aspects of the course, other than exams and quizzes, and how you feel your performance in these areas has been. I would like you to think about any problem areas which you for see arising which might adversely impact your performance in the class. Finally, I would like you to suggest ways in which you might deal with the potential problems you see and/or how I might be able to help through changes in the class procedure or activities.

The following questions serve as a guide to help focus your attention on aspects of the class which I would like us to review. Please do not limit yourselves to these questions. Add anything you feel is appropriate and will help me to better understand your performance in the class and how you perceive my role in the course.

- How do you feel your performance in the class has been so far?
- Have you had any particular problems with understanding the course content?
- Do you feel you have been able to devote sufficient time to this course?
- Are you satisfied with your approach to studying and preparing for class and exams etc.?
- Do you forsee any problems arising within the course structure or outside of the class which might have an adverse impact on your performance?
- What actions can you take to help yourself overcome any future problems?
- How do you feel your group is functioning on the collaborative exercises?

- What possible solutions are there to the problems identified above, which might involve your collaborative group(s).
- What is your opinion of the effectiveness of the class procedures, particularly the collaborative learning activities?
- Do you have any suggestions regarding the class procedure which would help the entire class succeed in the course?
- Do you have any suggestions which would assist me in helping you succeed in this class?
- Are there any other observations you wish to make, questions you wish to raise, or anything else you would like to add which I did not raise above?
- Is there anything you would like to discuss with me which you would prefer to not raise in a group or whole class discussion? You may do this in writing or we can make an appointment outside of class time.

Student responses:

When I first saw this assignment my heart sank and I thought here is one more nail in my school coffin, more work to do in less time. I have your exam next week plus an English essay due along with a paper and exam in psychology, and exam in U.S. History. All this on top of my job and family pressures. I think I have been in a state of denial, as my psychology professor might say, not wanting to think too much about any of these things. This writing assignment coming from my math class has served as a well needed wake-up call.

In answer to your questions I do feel that my performance has been good up to this point in the semester and I have surprised myself in how much I understand and remember all the rules and procedures needed to do algebra. My only problem now is the time crunch. I feel as though history is going to repeat itself and I am about to fall behind in many of my subjects. When this has happened before in math it has meant my doom. Once I get behind I never seem to be able to catch up and then I either fail or drop the course. I am determined not to let that happen this time! I have made up a study and work schedule for the next two weeks and will plant myself in the library in order to avoid the usual distractions. I will also talk to my family and let them know that they may have to fend for themselves for a while, until I am through this two week period. That will be a shock to them but I am sure they will survive. I have also arranged to get together with my group at Beth's house for a few study sessions prior to your exam. Two members of my group are also taking Psychology and History so we will use some of the time to study for those tests together also. That leads me to your other questions about how our group is functioning.

We have a pretty good group and work well together in class. We are starting to work much more out of class either in twos or more of us. With our busy schedules it is sometimes hard to get everyone together. As a suggestion perhaps you could spend some time in class having people compare schedules to make it easier to set up study groups. Also it would be great if you could pick a few times when you could be available on campus in case our group needed some extra help with something none of us could get. One of the things that I especially like about working in groups is that when someone falls a little behind there us usually someone else to help them back on track. This next two weeks may put that to the test.

In conclusion I want to say thanks, I think, for the wake-up call and the concern you have shown for our progress in this class. You seem to understand what we are going through and have a genuine interest in helping us help ourselves. Like the commercial said after a guy gets a slap in the face to get his attention, "Thanks, I needed that."

My progress in this course is amazing me. Before entering this course the word fail was written all across my face. Algebra was like the word death to me. I was scared to death actually. I haven't changed my approach to doing math so far. Math was always my favorite subject because I love working with numbers, but not letters. Since I have entered this course and actually know what I am doing I feel I can accomplish anything. Some parts are difficult but if I apply myself I can do it. My attitude has changed a little bit. I feel more confident about myself and my knowledge. It has given me a broader range of knowledge and has made me aware of my ability to learn. I don't really have any problems or concerns at this point as long as I keep up with every class and complete the assignments on time. I am generally pretty careful to allow enough time for this class since I know it will take me longer to understand the formulas and rules.

I believe the procedures you are using so far are done in a fun a spirited way that makes it easier to understand algebra. The class has life and I want to pay attention and learn. I want to be there every day and want to continue in this direction. I like working in groups since I have met several nice people and we are able to help each other. That makes the class interesting and the time just flies by. That is a new experience for me. Most classes drag on and I have trouble paying attention the whole time. I don't really have any suggestions to improve my group in class. One idea would be to get together outside of class to get ready for the tests or work on homework together. You stated in class that you would encourage this and it wouldn't be cheating. In high school we had to work on our own which compared to your methods was much harder. I feel good about myself because I want to learn. I am looking forward to hearing what other people have to say in class when we get together to discuss this writing assignment. I would like to get some new ideas about studying math and hear how other people are doing.

WAC - EXERCISE #2D

Mid semester Push or...How Do I Survive All My Professors Demands?

Description

The mid point of the term has arrived and the decibel level of student complaints, about their work load in all their classes, is noticeably rising. Mid term exams, projects, essays and various other assignments are all coming due at about the same time and your course is being left in the dust. Student enthusiasm for your material appears to be waning. How many of us have encountered a situation in our educational endeavors where we had two or three exams during the same day and wondered if our professors ever talked to each other or the students about exam schedules? How do you get your students attention back and keep them focused on your class?

This activity suggests that you ask them directly through a mid term push writing exercise which states the problem and any concerns you may have and asks the students for their help and suggestions. There are three aspects of the class which I ask students to reflect upon in order to call their attention to the pitfalls of midterm pressures and to solicit their ideas and commitment to investing additional energy in the class. The first asks their current attitude and what they need to do to reinvigorate themselves in the class. The second question asks them to reflect upon their relationship to their group(s) and how they can help and be helped by their peers. The third question asks how they see my role and how I can help them concentrate on course activities and content, including areas such as assignment and exam schedules.

This exercise alerts my students to a concern which I have which is based upon many years of experience and observations of student behavior. It also signals my interest in their success in the course and desire to involve them in the planning and operation of the class. It emphasizes my commitment to investing extra energy into the class on their behalf. It also enables me to open a dialogue with the class about a problem which arises every semester yet goes unrecognized by students and most professors.

As a writing assignment it is especially valuable because it causes students to think more carefully about the problem as they compose their responses. They often provide valuable suggestions about how course procedures, exam schedules and assignments can be modified to help alleviate some of the mid term sources of pressure. This exercise provides an excellent mechanism for communications between students and professor and often allows professors to help address other problems students may be dealing with which are non-academic in nature such as family or financial pressures etc. Students are often surprised and amazed at the level of introspection this exercise draws out of them and indeed it promotes a higher level of motivation by the student and professor.

Purposes

1. To call students' attention to a serious problem which occurs at the at the mid point of the term.

2. To involve students in making adjustments to course procedures and/or schedules at the midterm if needed.

3. To re-energize students and focus their attention on what behaviors they and the professor will need to exhibit in order for the class to be successful.

4. To open a line of communication between the professor and student which may be helpful in dealing with a student's particular problem(s).

Alternate Uses

1. This type of exercise may be assigned at any point in the semester to address a concern which the professor has regarding the course.

2. The exercise may be adapted to address specific changes in behavior or activity level of students during a semester.

3. This exercise may be used at any time during the semester to address a concern raised by students regarding outside or other pressures which are adversely affecting their performance in the course.

Implications/Application for Collaborative Learning Opportunities

1. Working in pairs students develop a list of the sources of pressure which are adversely affecting their performance in the class.

2. Working in groups students develop a schedule of assignments and exams for the remainder of the course.

3. Students develop a list of actions which they might take in order to deal with the problems identified in part one above.

4. Groups develop a list of suggestions for improving class procedures or activities.

MID-SEMESTER PUSH–OR HOW DO I SURVIVE ALL MY PROFESSORS DEMANDS?

At this point in the semester you may be feeling unusual pressure to complete many projects, papers and exams. I would like to help us through this part of the semester successfully. To that end I would like you to write about how you feel you are dealing with this course and what outside pressures may be distracting you from performing better. I would also like to find out from you how I may be of assistance in reinvigorating and refocusing your attention onto this class without sacrificing other classes. Please answer the following questions. Use the reverse side of the paper if more space is needed.

1. How would you characterize your attitude toward the class at this point in the semester in terms of how much time you are putting into it and how enthusiastic you feel about the class? What can you do to help motivate yourself or re-energize your participation in class?

_____

_____

_____

2. How is your group functioning? What can your peers do to assist you in meeting the course requirements? What can you do to assist your fellow group members and encourage their participation in the class?

_____

_____

_____

3. What can I (Ted) do to help you or your group focus your energy on this class? I would appreciate your constructive suggestions on areas such as exam schedules, class activities, group activities etc.

_____

_____

_____

4. Are there any other problems or concerns you have which you would like to bring to my attention personally, not be used in a general class discussion, which I might be able to provide some advice or assistance on? These may be of an academic or non-academic nature.

_____

_____

_____

Student responses:

Question #1

So far during the semester I have been able to keep up with the schedule and all the work requirements of the class. I have found that the working in groups has been a big help because when I get a little behind someone else can usually help me get back on track and when they fall behind I can help them. The past two weeks I have had much less time to put into working on algebra which worries me. I do my best when I can work on the material a little bit every day. I have two exams and a midterm paper due. My work hours have been increased from 20 to 30 hours, luckily I have the late shift at a gas station and can do some reading if business is slow. I will try to schedule more study time during my work hours and get together with my friends less until I complete all my work. I will also try to spend at least one hour per day doing math, even if it means sleeping less.

Question #2

My group is working pretty well together. There are times when some of the people in the group come to class unprepared which makes completing the assignment more difficult. I don't mind helping other students since I am sometimes guilty of not being prepared as well as I should when I get super busy at work or with my other classes. I am grateful when they help me get caught up. As a suggestion we might try calling each other at home to discuss class projects or set up a regular schedule to meet as a study group outside of class. I feel that just having other students else to talk to on a regular basis in class is helpful when we get to crunch time.

Another suggestion would be to have other students discuss with the whole class their strategies for dealing with all the work they have.

Question #3

I think this assignment is a good start. I'm glad to know that you are aware of some of the problems we have as students and how all the work gets to us sometimes. I like the idea of making the exam schedule somewhat flexible depending on what other work we have due on a particular day, as long as we don't fall behind the on the syllabus. I would suggest that we move on to new material before we take an exam on the already covered material and that we use study groups to do our review outside of class. Could you schedule specific times where you could either run a study group or be available to answer questions if we can't solve problems ourselves?

Question #4

The only area where I might run into trouble is with my work. As I stated before my work hours have been increased because someone else quit. My hours may be increased to 40 hours per week which would be great for the money but may reduce my study time. If I keep the late shift this will not be a problem but if I am moved up I will have much less time to study on the job. If I run into any problems with this I will talk to you about it. I may have to take an incomplete in the class and finish it over the break if that is possible, but I will hope for the best. So far the class has been going well for me and we only have seven weeks to go so if I keep working I am confident I will complete the class with flying colors. Thanks for calling our attention to the need for each of us to keep working as hard as we can for the rest of the semester.

FINAL SEMESTER PUSH

Description

You are entering the final third of the semester and begin to notice that your students are not working as hard as they were at the beginning of the semester. You hear a rising crescendo of student complaints about the workload from other courses. Term papers are coming due, essays need to be revised and resubmitted, projects and lab report deadlines are fast approaching. What can you do to refocus your students attention on your course without dictating terms or becoming more strident in your admonitions to the students? The answer lies in the "class meeting," an excellent cooperative learning activity which utilizes this writing assignment as a basis for creating a student generated success strategy for course completion.

Students often feel alone and isolated in their frustration over semester pressures. This activity helps create a learning community for the students and provides a system of support through the sharing of problems and brainstorming solutions in groups and as a whole class. Three questions are posed for completion by the students as homework. The writing assignment is completed individually first. The first question asks students to focus on themselves and what they need to do to insure their success in the course. Students are rarely asked to make a conscious decision about whether they wish to succeed in a course and how they might act to insure their completion of the course. The second question asks students to consider how the teacher might assist them. This might involve rescheduling assignments, projects, or exams, forming study groups or providing extra help sessions to name a few areas where teachers can impact student success. Finally they are asked to reflect upon how their working in groups could be utilized to help reinvigorate them for a final semester push. The last question is especially appropriate and helpful if collaborative learning methods have been used throughout the semester and students have become familiar with the benefits created by working together with their peers.

There are many possible follow up activities which would be useful in class. At a minimum students will refocus individually on their situations in the class and consider personal actions they might take to insure their success. The next activity might involve the students in reading their responses to the whole class followed by a general discussion on the outside pressures they are facing and what they need to do to deal with them. A general strategy usually emerges with helpful suggestions for the teacher and students. A list of helpful hints can be generated for class distribution. Finally, this assignment could be used for a collaborative exercise by asking groups to develop success strategies which they would share with other groups in a plenary class session.

Purposes

1. To help students deal with end of semester pressures generated by project deadlines and multiple exams.

2. To emphasize the importance of student planning and study habits to help insure their success in the course.

3. To serve as a tool to help motivate students.

4. To build a supportive classroom environment which facilitates student interaction and assistance of one another.

5. To demonstrate teacher empathy with the students end of semester problems and outside pressures.

6. To formulate success strategies which students would find helpful in all their courses.

Alternate Uses

1. The survey questions could be made more specific, such as "What do you need to do to complete a project or prepare for the next exam?"

2. The assignment might focus on what preparations are necessary for success on the final exam.

3. Additional questions could be added which ask students to reflect upon their performance to date and to project how well they would do for the remainder of the semester.

4. Students might be asked to evaluate their group's perfor-

mance and what they could do to facilitate better group interaction and performance.

Implications/Applications for Collaborative Learning Opportunities

1. In a class meeting model the entire class discusses the assignment, defines problems students are dealing with and develops a set of suggestions for themselves and the teacher.

2. As a follow up activity groups of 3-4 students may be asked to prioritize the list of suggestions based upon some criteria such as most helpful item, most likely to help, most effective suggestion, etc. This is followed by a plenary session to review each groups priority list.

3. If groups have been together throughout the semester the can be asked to develop a success strategy for the group based upon their priority list. This might include study groups, help sessions, working sessions, informal gatherings, etc.

FINAL SEMESTER PUSH FOR SUCCESS

Congratulations! We have finished two thirds of the semester successfully. At this point in the semester, based upon numerous comments, I am getting the feeling that some of us are running out of steam when it come to working on and studying for this class. This is a critical time in the semester. We have made it this far successfully. It would be a shame to let all that hard work go for naught.

There are other pressures building from other courses which make it harder to concentrate on this course. Therefore we need to develop a strategy to help us stay on track and even increase the momentum we have developed. Please take a few minutes to think about and answer the following questions. Be prepared to discuss your responses within your groups and with the whole class.

We will combine your suggestions with your classmates in an attempt to develop a success strategy which will carry us through to the end of the semester. Your suggestions will also help your classmates and you succeed in other classes as well.

Please type, print or write neatly. Keep your answers as succinct as possible. Short sentences or phrases would be ideal for later use in group or class exercises. Use the reverse side of the paper if you need more room.

1. What can you do to insure that you will finish this class successfully?

_____

_____

_____

2. What can I do to help, is your quest for success in this course?

_____

_____

_____

3. What can we do together (in groups) to get all of us through this class?

_____

_____

_____

WAC – EXERCISE #2F

END OF SEMESTER STUDENT SELF EVALUATION

DESCRIPTION

In the past I have felt very dissatisfied with how I have ended my classes. Something was always missing, that of having the students more involved in the process. I have tried using the last class to summarize the semesters material, made short speeches about my reactions to what transpired during the semester, and discussed and recommended follow up courses students might consider. I have tried having and end of semester celebration. All to no avail, the classes never felt complete. My attempts at closure were very one sided and did not involve the primary participants in the class, the students.

In order to rectify this situation and gain as much feedback and insight from the students I initiated an end of semester student self evaluation. In this exercise I ask the students to reflect upon their performance and reaction to the class and to make suggestions for improving the class. In addition they are encouraged to add any comments they feel are relevant, in a constructive way, to the class or my class procedures and activities. This assignment gives me n opportunity to ask specific questions such as how they felt about collaborative learning and what they would do differently if they had the class to do over again.

The responses are very satisfying to me. Students take the assignment seriously and often make important observations about their performance in and reactions to the class and what they might do in the future to improve. Their suggestions are very helpful to me and enable me to determine if particular collaborative learning activities are effective and well received or not. The fact that I have asked for their opinions and suggestions makes the assignment more consistent with the collaborative learning paradigm which we have used throughout the semester. In some classes I will request the exercise be completed prior to the last class in order to use it in a final group activity and brainstorming session.

Purposes

1. To encourage students to reflect upon their performance in the course and what actions they might take in future courses to improve their understanding of concepts.

2. To provide student feedback on their reactions to course procedures such as learning in groups and interactive activities.

3. To solicit suggestions from students about course procedures and activities.

4. To identify problems which have occurred during the semester which were not discussed previously or written about in other writing exercises during the semester.

Alternate Uses

1. Questions may be tailored to answer specific concerns of the professor.

2. Students who write about unique or specific problems they are having or have had, which have not surfaced during the class, may be contacted after the semester is completed or even before final exams are finished.

3. Student self evaluations might be useful for introducing the course in future semesters by providing student testimonials about the class. Students are generally very willing to share their observations if asked by a professor assuming that the material does not contain personal information.

Implications/Applications for Collaborative Learning Activities

1. This exercise must be completed prior to the end of the semester in order to have the information available for collaborative learning activities.

2. Pairs or larger groups discuss their self evaluations and outline what actions they would take to improve their performance.

3. Groups develop suggestions for improving future courses.

END OF SEMESTER SELF EVALUATION

I WOULD LIKE YOU TO DO AN EVALUATION OF YOURSELF IN RELATION TO THIS CLASS. THIS WILL NOT COUNT IN ANY WAY TOWARD YOUR GRADE, HOWEVER IT IS REQUIRED TO COMPLETE THE CLASS. PLEASE ANSWER THE FOLLOWING QUESTIONS, NOT NECESSARILY IN THE GIVEN ORDER. PLEASE FEEL FREE TO ADD ANYTHING ELSE YOU WOULD CONSIDER APPROPRIATE TO HELP ME UNDERSTAND HOW THIS COURSE WENT FOR YOU.

- HAS YOUR APPROACH TO MATH CHANGED DURING THIS COURSE FROM PREVIOUS COURSES OF EFFORTS IN MATH? IF YES HOW?
- HAS YOU ATTITUDE OR FEELING ABOUT MATH CHANGED? WHAT WERE THEY BEFORE VERSUS

NOW?
- HOW DO YOU FEEL YOU PERFORMED IN THIS COURSE?
- WHAT WOULD YOU DO DIFFERENTLY IF YOU HAD A CHANCE TO DO THIS ALL OVER AGAIN?
- WHAT ARE YOUR FEELINGS ABOUT USING GROUPS IN THE COLLABORATIVE LEARNING APPROACH TO STUDYING AND DOING MATH?
- WHAT DID YOU LIKE BEST ABOUT IT?
- WHAT DID YOU LIKE LEAST ABOUT IT?
- HOW MIGHT THE CLASS BE IMPROVED IN THE FUTURE?
- WHAT ARE YOUR FUTURE PLANS FOR MATH, IF ANY?
- WHAT ELSE WOULD YOU LIKE TO ADD THAT I DID NOT ASK

PLEASE TYPE YOUR EVALUATION

Students Responses:

In the past as you know, Ted, I have taken a class with you and have enjoyed your approach in learning the material. Before your classes I disliked math. I was always getting aggravated and scared by it. Working together with those around me in a group has been a great help in understanding the material and the many different ways in which a problem can be tackled and solved. For me the beauty was being able to work one on one with someone every day. I was constantly learning something new and leaving class feeling relaxed and in control. On those days I could not understand something I did not feel half as bad as I normally would have, I knew that if it were something I could not figure out at home or at the next class period I could count on receiving help.

If I had a chance to do it all over again I would do what I always say I am going to do at the beginning of the semester, and what I had wished I had done more of at the end of the semester, to do more math work at home by myself. With other classes, a job and still living at home it is hard. This semester was particularly hard for me. My grandfather got very sick and passed away a couple of weeks ago. For a couple of classes in a row I was absent and had difficulty keeping up with the material. I have visited the math lab recently and have received help there and am working on getting everything under way for the upcoming final.

My future plans are to hopefully pass this class and enter into my first credited math class next semester so that I may graduate from Cape Cod Community College in May. I am deciding on Statistics, Survey of Math or Business math. I only wish you were teaching one of these, then my decision would be easy. Wherever I transfer I will take Pre-calculus since I am majoring in Environmental Science. So it seems my road through mathematics is just beginning. That is all right since I plan to put a good amount of time into it. The hardest part for some people is just realizing their weaknesses and now since I have already done that I just need to do my best to change them.

Thanks again Ted for a great class and another wonderful learning experience.

Before I signed a contract with you Ted, I made a pact with myself to try to keep trying in algebra. I kept that pact. My math confidence went up at first, then it slid a bit. Then it went up again; but, I have never gone down to the point I was at once, which was to completely shut down. You have certainly had a lot to do with my "hanging in there." You have been patient and have tried to attend to everyone's confusions with your simple and direct style."

I was amazed that I am able to think through as much as I can with these problems. Although it was 26 years ago (in high school), I can remember feeling totally lost and hopeless. I don't feel that way any more. If only for that reason alone I think I performed well this semester in algebra.

I signed up for this class in June with a fairly set idea of what I should expect and how I would use this course to help me in future classes. I had taken algebra before but it was three years ago so I wanted to have a refresher course. I can honestly say that I was not looking forward to the class at all, but the material the teacher sent me prior to the beginning of the semester made me forget about any preconceptions I had about math courses. The course started very smoothly and it was easy to become adjusted to the style of teaching the instructor used.

The class itself was exactly what I was looking for in a math class and I found after a quick review of the material that I remembered it from high school. I found it was more of a math practice rather than a math class, with the class being made up primarily of peer aides and the teacher acting as more of a coach showing the students what they had been doing wrong or how they could do what they were doing right more efficiently.

All in all I am very pleased with what this course has given me. I find myself in a much better position to handle more advanced math and science courses. I plan to use my re-found knowledge of algebra before I forget it again, and not wait another three years before taking another math course.

When I re-entered school almost two years ago I was told that I needed to take an algebra course. I panicked. Even though I had taken a large number of math courses in high school I feared that I had forgotten everything I had learned so long ago. It was a pleasure to realize how much I truly enjoy working with numbers once again. The course was presented in a way that made learning and remembering fun.

3-GROUP PROCESSING

Interactive learning techniques based upon cooperative structures usually have social processing components to assist students in working together. Students generally do not have experience working in groups or collaborating on course assignments do to the competitive nature of our educational systems. The writing assignments in this section provide mechanisms for students to consider how their groups are functioning and what contributions they are making to the success of their groups. Students are asked to reflect upon the group process and what can be done to improve it. In addition it is helpful to show students what research has been published which validates the small group, interactive approach to learning and teaching. This is accomplished by asking students to review research articles reported in the New York Times and Boston Globe, which emphasize the value of students working together in small groups.

A- How can we work better in groups?

B- Encouraging student writing by example–Analysis of newspaper articles

C- Developing T-Charts to help analyze group functioning

D- How did we do today in out group?

HOW CAN WE WORK BETTER TOGETHER IN GROUPS

Description

Collaborative learning has been thoroughly researched and documented as an effective teaching/learning paradigm. In order to establish this approach professors need to work with students to help them become effective participants in groups and to have them consider how to make the process mutually beneficial when interacting with their peers. The social aspect of interactive learning is often misunderstood and therefore students need opportunities to reflect upon what is happening in their groups, how are they functioning, and what can be done to improve them.

This assignment is offered after students have been working in groups for 2-3 weeks. Prior to asking students to review their group's performance and their relation to their group they would have worked extensively in pairs and threesomes and would just be starting to work in groups of 4-5 members. When students work in pairs they are generally few problems because of the intensity of the interaction. One person explains their ideas and the other person listens and then offers comments or asks questions. When groups are enlarged potential problems surface because there is much more idle time. When one person is talking the other 2-4 group members may or may not be listening carefully. A typical problem results when larger groups break up into pairs even though an activity calls for everyone in the group to work together. Students need to have their attention focused on how they should be acting in their groups in order for the groups to be effective.

This exercise asks students to evaluate their personal reaction to working in groups, what things their group is doing well, and what could be improved. They are also asked to suggest a group size they feel would be most effective for them to work in, and to make specific suggestions about how they could help their group function better and what behaviors they would like to see evidenced by their group's members.

At this point in the term students will have had experience v. orking in groups ranging is size from 2-5 members. While they are certainly not experts in group dynamics they will have had enough experience, through class activities in group building, to know which behaviors assist groups and which interfere with a group's performance. When used as a basis for a collaborative class activity this exercise helps students establish appropriate behaviors. It also enables groups to identify any problems they may be having and to start the process of changing they way in which group members interact. Communication with the professor is also important as a way of evaluating whether the group structure is working well or whether changes in the make up of some groups is necessary.

Purposes

1. To provide a method for students to assess how they are functioning in their groups.

2. To encourage students to assess how well their groups are working.

3. To allow students to identify problem areas within their groups.

4. To provide a method for the professor to assess whether groups are functioning properly.

5. To provide a basis for altering group composition during the semester.

6. To solicit suggestions from students which will help their groups work better and thus involve them in setting up or modifying class procedures.

Alternate Uses

1. Have groups or individuals develop group exercises for use by the whole class.

2. Have students address specific problems which they discussed in the assignment or which he professor or students have observed in class.

Implications/Applications for Collaborative Learning Opportunities

1. Students read their comments to their groups and obtain feedback, questions or reflections from their peers.

2. Groups develop a list of appropriate and inappropriate group and individual behaviors.

3. The class develops a master list of helpful behaviors and activities to be used by individuals in their groups.

4. Groups outline a strategy for their groups to work better together. Strategies are then shared as part of a whole class discussion.

HOW CAN WE WORK BETTER TOGETHER IN GROUPS?

We have been working in groups of two or more people for several weeks. I would like to take some time to think about how this process is working and what we can do to make it work better. Please answer the following questions. Use the reverse side of the paper if you need more room.

1) How do you feel about working in groups up to this point in the semester? What activities are working for you and what could be improved? What size group do you feel is best for you (pairs, 3's, 4's etc.)?

2) What could you do to help your group work better? Please be as specific as possible. The focus of this question is on YOU, not the rest of the group or the professor. At least three ideas would be good and more would be helpful.

3) What actions or behaviors of your group's members would be most helpful to you?

4) What can I (Ted) do to help your group work better together?

Student Responses

1) How do you feel about working in groups up to this point in the semester?

My opinion on groups is that they are very helpful when everyone contributes. Not lot is working for me in my group.

If everyone did their work, maybe it would be different. Jill and I are always prepared for class but two other members are not. When that happens we just work in pairs instead of fours. A good group size is four.

2) What could you do to help your group work better?
    1. Be prepared for class.

    2. Go over problems with everyone in the group.

    3. Share information that you learned which is new to you.

3) What actions or behaviors of your group's members would be most helpful to you?
    1. Participation by all group members.

    2. Having each person explain what they are doing and how they answered the questions.

    3. Work in a more group-related fashion instead of everyone doing things on their own.

    4. Work together outside of class in study groups or in the math lab.

4) What can I (Ted) do to help your group work better together?
    1. Stress the need for everyone to work in their group.

    2. Change the people in each group more often so we can work with new people.

    3. Help us organize study groups outside of class.

    4. Check homework to make sure all the group members are prepared.

1) How do you feel about working in groups up to this point in the semester?
    I like working in groups. It gives you the chance to work things out together, what one person doesn't understand the other does. I think just a little more reinforcement from you would make me feel more confident in my ability. We have a group of five people who work real well together. If we are still having problems then we work together in the cafeteria or the math lab.

2) What could you do to help your group work better?
    Our group is working well together. We need to con-

---

tinue what we are doing. Personally I need to continue doing my work to be prepared, communicate with members in my group, help to explain a part to someone else if they don't understand, and ask for help if I don't understand something.

3) What actions or behaviors of your group's members would be most helpful to you?

The actions and behaviors of our group seem to right for us. We respect each others ability and do not make anyone feel bad if they are not getting it. We seem to be very supportive of each other. We also get together at lunch to go over things.

4) What can I (Ted) do to help your group work better together?

Since out group is working well I can't think of a lot of things you can do to help us. We really need to work things out ourselves. Maybe more assignments like this one which helps us to think about how we are doing would be helpful. You might want to look at some other groups which do not appear to be working as well as we are, but don't change our group. I know you want us to become as independent as possible but perhaps your could tell me more often when I am correct instead of asking my group members if they think I have the right answer.

GREAT IDEAS FOR HELPING OUR GROUPS WORK BETTER TOGETHER

Student responses obtained in a whole class discussion .
- Keep focused on the problem at hand during group work
- Continuity of grouping-keep the same groups during the whole semester
- Be open to help each other out with the math work
- Attending every class would help groups function better
- Get to class on time
- Form study groups outside of class
- Explain to others in the group how to do a problem if you understand it more than anyone else
- Encourage quieter students in the group to participate
- Be patient with each other and ourselves

- Offer to be study partners with other group members and go to the math lab
- Try not to feel funny when you have to ask for help
- Exchange phone numbers to have the opportunity to get together over the phone
- Alternate working steps in pairs to solve problems
- Share strategies for problem solving
- Be respectful of different speeds which people learn the material
- Repeat explanations if people do not get it right away
- All group members should be prepared for class
- Go over the material before class and discuss any questions with the group
- Basically members need to be hard workers
- Everyone should contribute equally to the group
- Keep the atmosphere somewhat light, but without clowning around
- Look over assignments before class
- Make sure everyone understands the solution before moving on
- Establish a buddy system
- Redefine our goals set in our contract with Ted
- Read examples from the book together more
- The more difficult the problem the more interaction there should be
- Keep focused on the problem at hand
- Learn more about the people in your group
- Stop group talking when the teacher or tutor is talking to the group or whole class
- Try to insure that at least one person in each group understands the material
- Take turns speaking and listening
- Have group members check and recheck solutions to problems
- Establish personal goals for completing the class and check periodically to see if everyone is meeting their goals

ENCOURAGING STUDENT WRITING BY EXAMPLE-ANALYSIS OF NEWSPAPER ARTICLES DESCRIBING HARVARD RESEARCH ON LEARNING IN GROUPS

Description

Encouraging students to write can be accomplished by sharing with them examples of writing which relate to specific experiences in their lives or which illustrate concepts related to course content or procedures and then asking them to review the articles and express their opinions about the subject matter covered. This writing exercise is intended to focus students' attention on the value and purpose of collaborative learning in small groups which has been documented by educational researchers at Harvard University. The medium used consists of newspaper articles from the New York Times. The level of writing, vocabulary and research used in the articles are highly sophisticated.

A collaborative process is used to initiate this exercise. Students are asked to read each article prior to class. Working in pairs, in class, students write a summary of each of the articles focusing on the content and conclusions of the articles. The product of this part of the exercise may vary from a paragraph to a page or longer and represents a writing assignment within and assignment combined with a collaborative activity. Students are then asked to review the articles critically in order to develop an opinion on the conclusions expressed in the articles. This part of the exercise may be assigned individually or using pairs.

Students will have been working collaboratively for 3-4 weeks when this assignment is given. At this point in the semester they are becoming more comfortable with the collaborative approach but many are not entirely convinced of its benefits. These articles provide a strong case for using this paradigm based upon several years of research carried out at a prestigious institution. Through a students written analysis and critique of this research it is possible not only to improve their critical thinking skills but also to help them assume an ownership of the collaborative learning techniques used throughout the course.

Another benefit of this exercise occurs when students are encouraged to raise concerns or ask questions about the collaborative learning approaches used and make suggestions about class procedures. This final aspect of the exercise demonstrates the value of collaboration at all levels including teacher-student cooperation, especially when student suggestions are incorporated into the class procedure.

Purposes

1. To demonstrate professional writing for students using course procedures as the topic.

2. To encourage students to think critically about writing examples, especially those dealing with course content and procedures.

3. To help students understand the research base for collaborative learning in order to emphasize the benefits of collaborative learning.

4. To create a stronger association between writing and collaborative learning within the students.

5. To foster a collaborative learning environment in the class and encourage student input into class procedures.

6. To provide a collaborative learning experience which will help students understand the nature and value of collaboration in an academic class.

7. To encourage students to write during class and outside of class using non-content subject matter.

8. To demonstrate and practice a pair-writing and editing process for students which might be useful in other courses.

Alternate Uses

1. Teachers may substitute their favorite article on research dealing with alternative teaching approaches or content subject matter.

2. This exercise may be expanded into a larger research effort where students are asked to find articles on teaching techniques, collaborative learning, or interactive learning approaches.

3. Content related articles may be used, especially in education related courses.

4. The assignment may be used to introduce pair-writing or pair-editing of peers writing in any course

5. These or other articles may provide a base for introducing students to collaborative learning paradigms instead of material taken from a textbook.

Implications/Applications for Collaborative Learning Opportunities

1. This exercise is primarily a collaborative learning experience using writing as it's basis. The procedures outlined above explain how the process can be applied in virtually any class using a variety of articles on collaborative learning, alternate teaching techniques or course content.

2. This exercise may be expanded to run over several classes with plenary session analysis and/or reading of pair and individual writing results.

3. Follow up activities are possible once students become familiar with the idea of pair-reading, pair-writing and pair-editing of their work. These may be encouraged both in and out of class.

4. For the more adventurous, pair exams or collaborative homework assignments may be used in place of individual tests on course content.

EVERYONE CAN BE A NEW YORK TIMES CRITIC

In this assignment you are asked to put yourself in the shoes of a New York Times education critic and review the articles attached on research carried out at Harvard University on how students learn best. Your work will form the basis for a collaborative learning exercise which is described below.

The purposes of the assignment are threefold. First to encourage you to think about the collaborative learning procedures we have been using in class; second to provide a collaborative learning exercise; and third to encourage writing in class with your peers. Each of these purposes are intended to help develop critical thinking skills which are fundamental to the class and your education in general.

Assignment Process

1. For homework, review each of the articles attached for content. Write a summary in your own words for each article.

2. During class you will join with a partner to discuss the articles and write a single review of each article describing the content and conclusions drawn by the authors. These will be submitted at the end of class. You may be asked to share your work with the class in a plenary session.

3. Continuing to work with your partner you will now critique each article orally, basing your analysis upon your experiences to date working in small groups in this class, and experiences you may have had in other classes where small groups and/or collaborative learning techniques were used.

Questions you may wish to consider in making your critique may include but are not limited to the following.

Do you agree with the conclusions presented?

Would you suggest any follow up research studies or alternate approaches?

Are you able to observe any of the benefits described in the articles in the procedures we use in this class?

Please describe how.

Can you suggest activities or procedures which would be helpful in facilitating collaborative learning in our class?

4. The final product will be a critique of each article written individually. You may share your work with your partner prior to final submission and pair-editing is encouraged out of class.

5. Volunteers will be asked to read their papers to the class

and a general discussion will follow on the nature of collaborative learning and whether it is effective in our class, and how it might be made better. .

THE NEW YORK TIMES-MONDAY MARCH 5, 1990

How To Learn In College: Little Groups, Many Tests

by Edward B. Fiske

Some relatively simple changes in teaching methods can produce significant gains in learning for college students, according to a study made public yesterday by Harvard University. The researchers reported that college students do their best in courses that include "frequent checkpoints" like quizzes, tests and oral exams. They also thrive, the study reported, when they do at least some of their studying in small groups rather than logging long solitary hours of study in a library.

The widely held myth that college students prefer courses where they are left alone to work on their own with relatively few exams or papers is just that, a myth." Prof. Richard J. Light of the Graduate School of Education and the Kennedy School of Government, who directed the project, said in an interview.

Mid-Course Corrections

Jeremy Sevareid, a sophomore who is majoring in history and government, said, "I had one class where we had papers due every three weeks. That meant we really had to have a handle on the material, and if we didn't, it showed immediately."

The researchers reported that faculty members also benefited from occasional feedback. They recommended that professors ask students to write a "one-minute-paper" at the end of each teaching session describing "the big point you learned today" and "the main unanswered question you still have." "Such an exercise helps the student to focus on the critical themes on the course and gives the faculty member the chance to make mid-course corrections in their teaching," Mr. Light said. The findings grew out of Harvard Assessment Seminars, a project initiated three years ago by Harvard's president Derek C. Bok, to promote more internal examination of teaching, advising and student life.

Organizing Their Thoughts

Noel Ignnatiev, an instructor in history and literature, said he tries to give his classes a short assignment every week. "When students have to write something–even if it is not graded–it compels them to organize their thought and take some responsibility for how the class goes," he said.

The first summary of the study, "The Harvard Assessment Seminars: Explorations With Students and Faculty About Teaching and Student Life," was made public yesterday. Here are several other findings:

• Students who devote a lot of time to intramural sports and other extracurricular activities have higher morale, but no lower grades than those who are less active. The only exception is members of varsity teams, who have slightly lower grade point averages than non-athletes.

• Contrary to widespread belief, faculty members are "willing." even eager to use new technology like computers and video discs, but their good intentions usually work only when professors are backed by an "expert" skilled in the use of technology in standard courses.

• Men and women contrast sharply in how the study and what they expect from college. Two-thirds of the men in the study but less than a quarter of the women said they wanted academic advisors who "make concrete and directive suggestions," the researchers reported. By contrast, nearly three-quarters of the women but only 30% of the men value advisors who "will take the time to get to know me personally."

As Teaching Was Faulted

The researchers also reported that male students' overall satisfaction with college was closely tied to how well they did academically, while that of women was "influenced far more by personal relationships and by informal encounters and meetings with faculty and advisors."

The seminars were created at a time of growing public criticism of the quality of undergraduate teaching at American colleges and universities. Education authorities in at least one state, Missouri, are requiring public universities to give tests of general knowledge to entering freshmen and to give similar follow up tests to determine how much the students have learned. The Harvard Assessment Seminars rejected this idea of trying to determine what students know in favor of determining the conditions under which students do best work. Instead of what the students know, the professors want to know what makes the processes more effective. trying to

ascertain students' historical perspective and literary sensitivity, for instance, is difficult to measure at the college level, especially with standardized tests.

Participants split into eight groups to conduct research on such topics as how to improve classroom teaching. Interviews were held with random samples of 365 Harvard undergraduates, and questionnaires and logs were kept by students on how they spent their time. More than 100 faculty members and administrators took part in the seminars, about half of them from Harvard and the rest from more than 20 other colleges. The major overall finding, Mr. Light said, was that "small changes in teaching format can lead to significant gains for students."

The Courses They Like

The researchers reported that students have "remarkably clear and coherent ideas" about the courses that they like and respect. They like courses that are "academically demanding" but also offer frequent opportunities to revise and improve their work as they go along, the study said. They learn best, it found, "when they have a chance to submit an early version of their work, get detailed feedback and criticism and then hand in a final version for a grade." Such an approach, the study said, is most readily applied in courses in which students write papers–but quizzes, tests, brief papers and oral exams will also work.

The Smaller the Better

The report emphasized that a "quick turnaround" was imperative. "Receiving the same information two or three weeks later simply doesn't help as much," it stated. The grades of students who studies alone were compares with those of students who studied in groups of four to six. Invariably, the researchers reported, "students who study in small groups do better than students studying alone." For example, in Moral Reasoning 30, "Jesus and the Moral Life," Prof. Harvey Cox gives three lectures a week; he then divides students into sections of about 20 each for another meeting led by graduate students to discuss that week's readings. In 1988, he also offered students the option of attending sessions made up of five students who took turns leading the group with faculty members on hand. The report said videotapes of the various sessions showed that students in relatively small groups spoke more often, asked more questions and were generally "more engaged" than those in larger groups.

It was suggested that faculty members organize study groups. The researchers said that, "students should think twice if they find themselves spending all their study time working alone." "When lots of people are throwing out ideas, it helps you see different paths," said Sanjiv Kinkhabwals, a junior who is majoring in applied math. "In studying the humanities, I don't find it useful, because I need to read things by myself to understand them."

THE BOSTON SUNDAY GLOBE-NOVEMBER 10, 1991

HARVARD STUDY SAYS 1-ON-1 CONTACT AIDS STUDENTS

By Anthony Flint

Small classes, study groups and one-on-one contact with faculty and advisers are all key to a successful college experience, according to a new report by Harvard University. "Nearly every student with strong academic performance can point to specific activity that ties academic work closely to another person or a group of people," said Harvard education professor Richard Light, chief author of the report.

The report, based on interviews with 570 students, is the second installment of results from the Harvard Assessment Seminars, an effort begun five years ago on teaching, learning and the undergraduate experience. For more effective learning, the report said, students should mix large, required lecture courses with at least one small class per semester, and professors should organize classes into small groups, emphasizing the "interpersonal nature of academic involvement," Light said. "Putting it in negative terms, to come to Harvard or any other college and select four large classes each semester and drift quietly and anonymously in and out, to sit in a section quietly, and to study alone- maybe that will work for a few people, but students report overwhelmingly the opposite," Light said.

"One effective way to prompt interaction is to have students read each other's assigned papers, and discuss them in class," Light said. "In general the more writing, the more engaged the student," Light said. The report also found that one-on-one contact with faculty advisers was important, but many students did not feel comfortable approaching professors for informal discussion. Informal contact–a talk over coffee or chatting after class–is often the most important to students.

The Harvard Assessment Seminars are viewed as a model for teaching and learning methods at colleges and universities. The first report, released in March 1990, suggested that professors give one minute quizzes regularly to monitor the students. That has been adopted at some colleges.

WAC - EXERCISE # 3C

Developing T-Charts to help students analyze how groups function well

Description

An important aspect of cooperative learning involves helping students understand how groups function and what to look for in successful groups. Socialization is an important yet often overlooked part of a student's academic preparation. Employers express interest in employees who are able to work in teams with their peers on projects which require group brainstorming. What better place is there than within the safety of a college classroom to provide this training and practice.

T-Charts provide a mechanism for students to focus on what is going on in their groups by asking them to identify what a desired behavior would look like and sound like to an outsider observing the group in operation. A two column format is used with student suggestions about what one would observe in a group which was functioning well on one side and what they would expect to hear within the group on the other side. Students are asked to complete the forms individually and then share their observations with the larger group. Finally a master list is developed using input from all the groups ion the class. This master list becomes the model by which all the groups should operate.

An advantage of this form of group processing is that the preferable traits are generated by the students and may be used as classroom rules of decor. Teacher generated rules or procedures are less effective since they are often imposed upon students by an external power source. In addition students have a formal listing of ideal behaviors to refer to when dealing with their peers who may not be living up to good group behaviors.

Purposes

1. To help students focus on group behaviors which will facilitate good group interactions.

2. To encourage students to develop a code on conduct for their groups.

3. To involve students in establishing class procedures and appropriate reactions to students who do not contribute to group processes.

4. To highlight a series of potential problems associated with group interactions and work toward solving these problems by developing a consensus of the group.

5. To provide a visual guide to good group functioning. Lists of characteristics may be placed around the room on posters as a reminder to students or particular items may be emphasized from week to week.

Alternate Uses

1. Students might be asked to write a manual on good group functioning characteristics to be used throughout the semester to help their groups function better.

2. The master lists may be used to help students observe their group as it functions or to observe other groups with the idea of making constructive suggestions for better group performance.

Implications/Applications for Collaborative Learning Opportunities

1. Students work individually initially to develop characteristics of good group behaviors and then come together in their groups to share their observations. A Round Robin structure would be appropriate here. In this activity each student contributes one item at a time until all their observations are completed, avoiding duplication. The Round Robin can then be run with the entire class by receiving suggestions from each group, one at a time. After the list is completed a final review is made and accepted by the whole class.

WHAT ARE EFFECTIVE GROUPS LIKE

SOUNDS LIKE   LOOKS LIKE

STAYING ON TASK
ENCOURAGING
EQUAL PARTICIPATION
CRITICIZING IDEAS NOT PEOPLE
TAKING TURNS
BEING RESPONSIBLE
STAYING WITH THE GROUP
CONTRIBUTING IDEAS
PRAISING/NO PUT DOWNS

LOOKS LIKE

- People look busy
- One person is talking to the group and the other people are listening
- People are facing each other
- Everyone is sitting at the table versus sitting sideways or with their backs to the table
- Interested in one another
- People are sharing materials
- Some people may work in pairs and then work with the whole group
- People look prepared, they have problems worked out or written assignments completed

SOUNDS LIKE

- People are sharing ideas with each other
- People sound enthusiastic but not loud
- There is laughter in some groups
- One person is talking at a time
- Different group members ask questions of the group
- Discussion is focused on the subject
- People are talking about their experiences with the subject in previous classes
- Students may be discussing real life experiences and problems they have concerning their approach to studying or preparing for exams, etc.

4-CONTENT/ PERSONAL REFLECTION

Research on adult learning strategies has identified a key element to motivating students by having them relate their personal life experiences to course content. This section provides a number of assignments which ask students to call upon previous experiences to answer questions such as: why study a subject (in this case algebra); finding analogies to course content; course portfolios and journals. In journals students are asked to make personal observations, ask questions, or comment upon course procedures. Here they may include any material which may be pertinent to the course but which may not be identified as such by the instructor.

Finally, asking students to write poetry about a class often brings out the affective nature of learning and encourages students to express themselves in a different manner than they are used to. Poetry writing, as well as the above assignments, often opens up a new and different line of communication between the instructor and student.

A- There is a poet in all of us

B- Student course portfolio

C- Why study math?

D- Assessing students and yourself using the "one minute paper"

E- Finding analogies in life to clarify course concepts

F- The diary of a student or writing a course journal

THERE IS A POET IN ALL OF US

Description

I think that I shall never see a mathematical equation as lovely as a tree. Naturally I couldn't resist trying to get your attention by using (abusing) a famous line from the poem "The Tree" by Joyce Kilmer. Poetry can be used as a powerful tool to unlock a student's inner thought about their relation to a course or course content. In algebra classes where math anxieties are prevalent the use of a poetry writing assignment encourages students to make connections between algebra and their daily lives in a way they would not otherwise consider. Students who feel they have a stronger interest in writing versus math are often intrigued by the results of this exercise when their they see how their poems and those of their classmates give them insights into how different people deal with math anxieties.

This assignment provides me with important information about how students are handling the class, what concerns they have about themselves or my class procedures, what outside pressures they are dealing with, and how seriously they are taking the class. It also gives me some insight into the student's writing ability and thus indirectly a measure of their ability to read and understand mathematical concepts. Research has shown that one of the strongest indicators of success in math is a students reading level.

Students often find it easier to write about their concerns rather than to address a professor directly. When students take the time and make a good effort to compose a poem they often reveal much more about themselves than they might in conversation or during class discussions. They also appreciate the idea that someone is interested in their ideas and artistic abilities as well as their math skills. This avenue of communication is mutually beneficial to the students and professor and often leads to a stronger commitment and effort by the students.

Purposes

1. To help students make connections between course content and/or procedures and an artistic form of expression.

2. To provide an unusual form of communication between the student and professor.

3. To add variety to the class through an assignment which is not typical for that class, i.e. writing poetry in a math class.

4. To enable students to share their concerns and thoughts about their anxieties about the course or course content.

5. As a corollary to number 4, poetry enables students to share their interest and/or excitement about the class with the professor and their peers.

Alternate Uses

1. Students write a poem using course content as the basis instead of personal observations.

2. Create a class poetry book composed of the individual entries.

3. Use the poems as a basis for advising or counseling students who indicate they are having problems with the class.

Implications/Applications for Collaborative Learning Opportunities

1. Students read their poems in pairs or larger groups.

2. Students read each others poems to the class.

3. Working in pairs or larger groups compose a new poem.

4. Groups organize poems by topic structure or some other criteria as if they were editing a poetry book.

5. Groups use the poetry to identify problems students are having with the class, course content, or outside problems which adversely effect their performance. Whole class discussion follows this activity.

WRITING ASSIGNMENT - THERE IS A POET IN ALL OF US

I would like you to write a poem about math. You may use any form of poetry you wish such as free verse, rhyming, haiku or other form you prefer. You may write about your experiences with math in this class or other classes, your feelings about math or problems your are having, or a math problem, if one can be translated into poetry.

Use your imagination and release your thoughts from the algebraic rules and operations we have been concentrating so hard on in class, unless you "See a mathematical expression as lovely as a tree."

Student responses:

ODE TO MS. ALGEBRA

When I was a child, mother often said "Mind your P's and Q's."
Now I'm simply payin' my dues.
There's this real tough dude, he kinda looks like old Kris Kringle,
Believe it not. ALGEBRA makes him tingle!
When I was a child polly meant a bird who wanted a cracka.
This dude wants me to learn to facta.
Mono was a disease, not one instead of three's.
Bi well we all know what that means.
X stood for a kiss at then end of a letter.
But wait it gets better!
When I was a child we used to eat PI, ski down SLOPES, Flip pancakes not fractions, and damn we could CANCEL anything.
Ted, that's the dudes name,
well he's running a new game.
Minus is not subtraction it means negative.
Math is where we take English.
When I was a child Mother said I was backwards, I'm sure proud to say "Mom the world caught up to me."
Now if I could simply PASS this crazy course with a P
Because the next time I hear the alphabet.
I will surely flee.

MATH DOESN'T COME EASY TO ME

Math doesn't come easy to me.
It's not like my A, B, C's.
1+2+3 equals 6
But what does 2A + 6AB mean?
In life we use adding, subtracting.
multiplying, and dividing:
To answer everyday problems.
But I've never come across a day,
when algebra and geometry meant anything.
The two seem to have no meaning in life.
So why do professors waste their time teaching?
But I will accept, and try not to fret.
Because math doesn't come easy to me!

ALGEBRA POEM

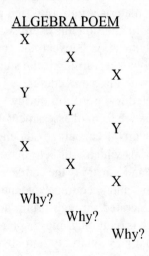

STUDENT COURSE PORTFOLIO

Description

During the semester students develop a variety of study methods and class materials which they use to understand the course concepts, study for exams and complete other course requirements. They often treat each activity as a separate and independent action. A student course portfolio is a mechanism designed to help students organize their materials into a unified and interrelated approach to the course. In addition this exercise provides an alternative means of communication between the student and professor and may serve to provide a warning if the student is having difficulties or problems with class procedures.

I introduce the course portfolio during the final third of the semester as an alternative form of assessment instead of relying on the standard hour exams. I encourage student to include in their portfolios any materials which will help them demonstrate to me that they understand and can apply the course concepts. I provide a list of suggested items and encourage students to use their imagination. Materials generated through group activities are acceptable. One item which is required is the chapter exam which is used to promote individual accountability and counts as an important element of the portfolio.

The portfolio is intended to broaden and expand the information I have available to evaluate student performance. The chapter exam serves as the starting point in the evaluation process. Next, in order to complete the evaluation, I look at homework assignments, in class work, text or class notes, flash cards, course journal writing and other assignments given during the semester period under consideration. I use all this information to assign a grade.

There is a certain amount of subjectivity in this process because I do not quantify the grading for journal entries as this would tend to limit students imagination. I use the journal evaluation to raise or lower chapter exam grades.

I assign the portfolio during the last third of the semester versus starting immediately because I want the students to become comfortable and familiar with my class procedures which include writing assignments, collaborative learning activities and many interactive class exercises. Also, by this time in the semester students will have accumulated a variety of materials which I would like them to organize more effectively. The portfolio could be assigned at the beginning of the semester as well.

Students find the portfolio concept of evaluation to be very encouraging and helpful. In addition to teaching them how to organize their materials they appreciate the opportunity the portfolio gives them to demonstrate their competence in a variety of ways. In math courses especially, where there is a high level of anxiety, students are enthusiastic about communicating how they have spent their time working on course content. They prefer a grading system which does not base its grade solely on as fifty minute exam.

Purposes

1 To provide information to the professor which will enable a more complete student assessment and grading process.

2. To help students organize a variety of course materials into a useful format.

3. To encourage students to review all their course materials within a unified context.

4. To allow students to demonstrate course proficiency through a variety of mechanisms.

5. To provide an avenue of communication between the professor and student during the semester.

Alternate Uses

1. Students review previous work completed during the semester in preparation for the final exam.

2. Students develop a portfolio of materials to bring forward to the next course.

3. Provide a portfolio for employment purposes. The material may be used as part of a resume or as backup material.

Implications/Applications for Collaborative Learning Opportunities

1. Groups develop a list of items which would be appropriate for inclusion in the portfolio.

2. Develop a master list of portfolio items through a whole class consideration of each group's suggestions.

3. Groups develop grading criteria for the portfolios including quantity of materials, quality levels, grade assignment, etc.

4. Groups or pairs review each other's portfolios for completeness and whether they meet the grading criteria.

MASTERY DEMONSTRATION PORTFOLIO

In order to demonstrate that we have mastered the material presented in chapters 11, 12 and 14 (time permitting) we are going to develop a mastery portfolio. This will include enough materials to prove that you know the material required. Suggestions for things to be included in the portfolio are as follows:

- Anything you feel will show me that you understand how to do the operations described in the chapter section.
- Completed problems from the exercises at the end of each section.
- Problems worked out in class on worksheets or in groups, presented in legible form.
- Copies of your 3x5 flash cards or notes
- Your written summary of each chapter section if that is what you use to study from.
- Materials gleaned from the math lab or obtained from getting tutoring help.
- Sample mastery demonstrations completed as take home exercises.

WHAT HAVE I LEFT OUT THAT WILL HELP ME DETERMINE WHETHER YOU HAVE LEARNED THE MATERIAL UNDER CONSIDERATION?????

Students Responses:

Table of contents from typical student portfolios
1. Chapter test
2. Chapter test corrected
3. Chapter homework
4. Review sheet with necessary formulas
5. Writing assignments
> Book section on how to solve word problems
> Poetry in math
> How did the quadratic equation come to be
> a short story
6. In class group assignments
7. Sample test developed by the group/plus answers to sample test
8. Flash cards used for studying important formulas and procedures
9. Observations and comments about personal performance, problems and successes during classes
10. Questions which occur after class or when doing homework

WAC - EXERCISE #4C

WHY STUDY MATH?

Description

Writing in math classes and collaborative learning activities create a synergistic environment within which students are encouraged to answer the age old question "Why do I need algebra?" Rather than attempting to impose my reasons for the value of studying math upon the students I shift the burden of proof to the student. In doing so I reduce the level of denial which occurs when I as the professor and authority figure try to convince a sometimes unwilling audience of the benefits of math and raise the level of ownership by the students. Students are generally surprised and impressed by the sheer number of reasons they articulate for studying math, when working collectively, whereas individually they may only describe at only a few reasons.

This exercise is intended to provide a degree of motivation for students who often bring to the class a high level of anxiety which causes skepticism about the need and value of studying mathematics. This is accomplished when students focus on their personal experiences with the usefulness of math. The collaborative element of the exercise encourages students to discuss the myriad of reasons for studying math among themselves in a safe environment. This is followed by discussion in a plenary class session. The power of collaboration is also demonstrated through this exercise as the students observe how the data base for reasons expands through each level of discussion.

Initially students are asked to work independently on the assignment as a homework exercise. Next they are arranged into groups of 3-4 and asked to develop a master list of reasons using a Round-Robin technique where each student offers a single reason followed by the next student working around the group until all members have completed their list of reasons. The final activity involves a plenary session of the whole class. A Round Robin technique is used here also with each group offering one reason, rotating among the groups.

Purposes

1. To create a connection between WAC and collaborative learning techniques.

2. To demonstrate the power of groups in brainstorming information and contributing to the class as a whole.

3. To help motivate students by identifying reasons they have for studying the subject matter.

4. To attach real life significance to the subject as observed by students.

5. To foster group interdependence and coherence using a non-content based subject.

Alternate uses

1. This question may be applied to any subject matter or course. Students often raise this question in any class which they

are required to take or which is a prerequisite for other courses.

2. Alternate questions may be substituted, such as: "Where have you observed math playing an important role in a decision making process?" or "Has math ever played an important role in your life?" etc.

Implications/Applications for Collaborative Learning Opportunities

This exercise uses a series of activities which culminate in a class listing of reasons students have for studying math or other subject as follows.

1. Students use the following worksheet to create their own list of reasons for studying math. This is done as a homework assignment.

2. Groups of three or four students are formed and asked to use a Round Robin approach to combining their individual lists. Each group expected to develop a consensus list by discussing each members contribution to determine if it belongs on the group list.

3. A plenary discussion concludes the exercise by again using a Round Robin method where each group contributes one item from their group list going around the class until all groups have contributed all their items, without duplicating items.

4. The master list is then recorded and duplicated for each member of the class

GROUP ASSIGNMENT- WHY STUDY MATH?

This assignment will be done in three parts.

Part 1- I would like you to develop a list of reasons why you feel it is necessary or important to study math. This is not meant to be a judgmental analysis but a personal assessment on your part based upon your life experiences. Your reasons should be in sentence form using brief sentences. You do not need to prioritize your reasons. This assignment is to be completed outside of class.

Part 2- In class I would like each group to compile a master list of reasons. To accomplish this we will use a Round Robin approach. Each student will contribute one item at a time moving

around the group until everyone has contributed all their suggestions. Be careful to avoid duplication.

Part 3- We will repeat part 2 with the class as a whole again
using a Round Robin technique with each group contributing an
item.

Reasons for studying math.

1._____
2._____
3._____
4._____

Student responses

Group 1- individual responses:

Student 1

    1. Math is used for general knowledge.

    2. It will be found in every form in the work force.

    3. Math is used when you go shopping.

    4. I use math when I use my computer.

    5. Math is helpful to pay bills, do my taxes and checkbook.

    6. I need math to get into a four year school and for my major.

Student 2

    1. Math exists in everyday life, from looking at the scale in
the morning and calculating how much weight one has gained, to
balancing your checkbook.

    2. Using your mind keeps it sharp and math does that.

    3. We couldn't colonize outer space without it.

    4. I need math to satisfy my degree requirements.

Student 3

    1. Math is used in our daily lives

    2. It is important to be able to perform tasks such as balanc-
ing a checkbook, paying bills, buying cloths, food and budgeting
your weekly pay for these expenses.

    3. It is required for my major.

    4. It is important to learn that math isn't always hard or that
we can like to do math.

    5. I need math to get into a four year college.

GROUP #1- COMBINED LIST
1. Math is needed for general knowledge.
2. Math is used in every form in the workplace.
3. Math is needed to pay bills, taxes and to use checks.
4. We use math for budgeting our expenses.
5. A college degree requires math.
6. Shopping for food, clothing, sales, coupons or whatever uses math.
7. Knowing math prevents you from being cheated out of your money.
8. All types of banking requires math.
9. Math can be fun to do.
10. Thinking logically keeps the mind sharp.
11. Math is needed for computer work.
12. Math is used in the following careers: Engineering, construction, architecture, science etc.
13. The more math you learn the easier it gets.
14. Math is helpful when playing games, knowing the odds of getting the right answer such as in the lottery etc.
15. When you get good at math your self esteem goes way up.
16. It is nice to be smarter than your kids so you can help them with their math instead of the other way around.

COMBINED CLASS LIST DEVELOPED IN A PLENARY SESSION
1. Math can be fun if it is made interesting.
2. Balancing a checkbook.
3. Paying bills.
4. Math provides the logic needed to work on computers.
5. Orders of operations are important in doing your taxes.
6. Helping other people with math problems.
7. Doing measurements (building, household etc.)
8. Math is important if you want to make money.
9. The field of architecture requires a lot of math.
10. To prevent yourself from being cheated out of money.
11. Budgeting your income.
12. To become smarter than your kids.

---

13. For cooking and changing recipes (fractions).

14. Degree requirements.

15. In the workplace everywhere.

16. For your self esteem.

17. The more you learn the easier it gets.

18. To make travel plans of all kinds (time management especially and finances).

19. Science requires high level math.

20. Engineering requires math.

21. Math helps in any job.

22. Making investments requires predictions and statistics.

23. Shopping where coupons are used and sales are held.

24. Prerequisites for other courses (statistics, nursing, business, etc.)

25. Liquor sales in counting the drinks per bottle, number of customers, etc.

26. Car performance in setting the timing, gallons per mile, etc.

27. Space travel needs accurate calculations.

28. Calculating tips both in getting them and giving them.

29. Playing pool uses a lot of geometry and angles.

30. Playing games- knowing the odds of success, especially in card games.

31. It helps you with different sports.

32. Betting, such as in the lottery or bingo games.

33. To make your life easier.

34. Math helps you understand why things happen.

35. To understand how mechanical things work.

36. Math is needed to transfer to a four year college.

37. It is very important in careers like space travel and exploration and astronomy.

38. It helps in getting a good job.

WAC - EXERCISE #4D

ASSESSING STUDENTS AND YOURSELF USING THE ONE MINUTE PAPER

Description

Standardized tests using multiple choice, true false, fill in the blanks or essay questions provide a limited basis for understanding and evaluating student performance. These methods deal primarily with factual information, rote memory and perhaps some critical thinking through an essay. What is needed in addition to these historic assessment techniques are methods for understanding students' affective learning skills and a variety of student learning styles. The "One Minute Paper," developed by Weaver and Cottrell(1), modified by Wilson(2) provides an excellent addition to our repertoire of assessment techniques.

The One Minute Paper is completed by the students at the end of class (and actually takes several minutes). Two questions are asked: (1) What is the most significant thing you learned today? (This question can be generalized as "What did you learn today?" or made case specific by asking "What did you learn about _____ today?"); (2) What question(s) do you still have? (This question may be left general or directed to a particular part of the class or concept.) The papers may be anonymous or signed. I recommend anonymous papers initially. This encourages students to participate more openly and provides general information for the teacher. Students will give more direct and honest answers if they feel they will not be judged or penalized by expressing their opinions and feelings. When students become familiar with this form of self assessment and learn to trust the teacher's response you can ask for signed papers. The primary advantage of a signed paper is that the teacher can respond directly and privately to individual students. A transition might involve making signatures voluntary for those students who wish a specific response.

The purpose of this exercise is to encourage students to reflect on the class and review and synthesize what they learned before they leave the class. Most classes end when the teacher has finished lecturing. It is an abrupt end causing students to focus on their next class or activity, virtually blocking out the material they have just covered. The next time they look at the material occurs when they start their homework.

Purposes

1. To have students summarize and synthesize the concepts covered by describing them in their own words. Teachers can then determine if students have understood the concepts covered in class.

2. Students review and focus on the most important ideas covered during the class.

3. They practice writing about the class content from their own perspective.

4. Students are asked to articulate what they do not understand. This helps them identify areas for further study and review.

5. Using a nonverbal approach, they can communicate their concerns, identify problems, ask for specific help, explain what is working for them and make suggestions for improving the class process. By responding to students in writing and verbally, teachers can personalize the process of teaching.

6. To help teachers determine if students understand the important concepts covered in class during each session. This approach provides immediate feedback to the teacher. They can identify problems individuals are having and whether they are widespread or individualized

7. A line of communication is opened between the teacher and students.

8. To use students' responses to provide ideas for improving instruction or call attention to a need for a review of material.

9. Teachers get to know their students much better. They get to know their students' personalities, problems, accomplishments as well as any extenuating circumstances behind poor student performance.

10. This technique can be used in large classes to obtain quick feedback in a short period with limited effort well before using an exam.

Alternate Uses

1. Instead of using generalized questions specific content areas may be explored using questions such as "What procedures are there to factor polynomials?," "Explain what you learned in class about different learning styles.," or other case specific questions.

2. Similarly in part two questions may be requested about a specific topic instead of left general.

3. In addition to the first two questions students may be given an opportunity to comment on other aspects of the class such as the course structure, class procedures, exam schedule, content, etc. through the addition of a third section of the One Minute Paper

Implications/Applications for Collaborative Learning Opportunities

1. Students work in pairs and exchange their papers in order to compare and discuss their responses.

2. They might try to answer each others questions. This idea can be extended to groups of 3 or 4.

3. Students individually or in groups could suggest questions and then analyze the collective responses and present the results to the class.

4. Groups could discuss problem areas identified by the above analysis and suggest solutions which might include changes in class procedures, student participation or other classroom issues.

References

Weaver, R. L., & Cotrell, H. W. (1985 Fall/Winter). Mental aerobics: The half-sheet response. *Innovative Higher Education, 10*, 23-31

Wilson, R. C. (1986 March/April). Improving faculty teaching: Effective use of the student evaluations and consultants. *Journal of Higher Education 57*(2), 196-211

K. Patricia Cross, & Thomas Angelo, *Classroom Assessment Techniques- A handbook for Faculty* 1988, prepared for the National Center for Teaching To Improve Post secondary Teaching and Learning

THE ONE MINUTE PAPER

PLEASE ANSWER EACH QUESTION IN ONE OR TWO SENTENCES

1) What was the most useful/meaningful thing you learned during today's session?

_____

_____

_____

2) What questions(s) remain uppermost in your mind as we end this session?

_____

_____

_____

3) (optional) Add any additional comments about your performance to date or other aspect of the class which has been on your mind. Constructive criticism as well as positive comments or helpful observations are welcome.

_____

_____

_____

Student Responses

1) What was the most useful/meaningful thing you learned during today's session?

- I learned the importance of doing things in sequence.

- I finally grasped the order of operations by practicing problems in my group.

- I realized that my sophomore math teacher was right! This stuff is actually interesting.

- I do remember this material and I just need to take my time and refresh my memory.

- Today I learned what quotient means, I've always wondered what it meant.

- Today I learned that the value of zero is a bonified answer! I also learned to do everything in parenthesis first and not to skip writing them.

- I learned that I can remember what I learned previously in elementary algebra with a little prodding.

- Use of the point-slope and intercept formulas for drawing graphs became much clearer after doing them in class today.

- The most meaningful thing I learned today was graphing. The reason being that from past experiences in math classes the graphing topics end up repeating in harder and harder forms throughout the book.

- How to solve equations better and how to have more practice with polynomials.

2) What question(s) remain uppermost in your mind as we end this session?

- Will I ever retain all of this material?

- What is uppermost in my mind is whether I will retain what I think I have learned today.

- What is the absolute value of something?

- When you have negative numbers used together like -6 -6. When you make the second 6 negative you take away the operation, so how do you know what to do with it?

- None, I understand everything that we did today.

- I still have a hard time with word problems.

- We haven't done division of polynomials before. You seemed to think that this was covered in the last class.

- How do I remember when to use the exponent rules when adding and multiplying polynomials. I keep mixing them up.

- I don't really have any questions except how I will do on the test?

- Why are there two equations for the slope? $m = (y1-y2)/(x1-x2)$ and $y-y1 = m(x - x1)$

FINDING ANALOGIES IN LIFE TO CLARIFY COURSE CONCEPTS

Description

Teaching which encourages students to make connections with their own experiences helps them to better understand and retain difficult concepts. This is true in general for all courses and especially appropriate in mathematics instruction.

In algebra the process of multiplying polynomials is relatively straight forward
and repetitious once the student learns the basic rules for adding and multiplying polynomials. The concept of factoring appears much more complicated because of the variety of factoring techniques available. Yet the concepts are closely inter-related where factoring is accomplished by division which is verified by multiplying the result, similar to arithmetic division being checked through multiplication.

In this exercise students are first asked to explain how multiplying polynomials and factoring are opposites. They must give their description in English without using math symbols. Next they are asked to describe a situation in nature or their lives that is analogous to factoring and multiplying. As you will see from the student responses there is a very strong critical thinking element brought out throughout this exercise. Students must first articulate the concepts in English in their own words and then consider a variety of activities which may or may not resemble the concepts and then write a description of their real life example. The process of writing about their experience involves a high degree of critical thinking and organization. In addition, when students have completed their work they generally have expressed a high degree of satisfaction of their understanding of the concept.

Students often express the feeling of frustration at the start of the exercise because they are not used to thinking about math in English terms, but as they work through the exercise they begin to have fun with it as they see more and more analogies. It is helpful to brainstorm analogies in class, either prior to starting the exercise or after the students have made one attempt at finding their own analogies. The group brainstorming serves to break the ice and initiate the thinking process which is necessary to complete the exercise.

Purposes

1. To encourage students to make connections between math concepts and real life situations.

2. To foster critical thinking through writing by asking students to describe natural phenomenon or their life experiences as related to course content.

3. To encourage students with strong writing skills to apply those skills to mathematics. Students often feel they are good at math or English but not both. This exercise helps to dispel that notion.

Alternate Uses

1. The concept of finding analogies or opposites based upon course content and real life circumstances can be applied to any academic course where there are definitive contrasts.

2. Specific analogies may be solicited through questions such as: "How is the brain like a computer and how is it different?" for psychology; "How does carrying out a science experiment mirror real life and how is it different?" for science classes.

Implication/Applications for Collaborative Learning Opportunities

1. Pairs of groups share their analogies with each other.

2. Groups may be trained in brainstorming techniques to assist individuals in finding analogies.

3. Groups might be asked to develop a list of analogies for presentation to the class.

4. Groups may be asked to formulate new analogy questions for the class to evaluate.

FINDING ANALOGIES IN OUR LIVES TO HELP UNDERSTAND THE CONCEPT OF FACTORING AND MULTIPLYING POLYNOMIALS

The purpose of this writing assignment is to help us better understand factoring of polynomials by making connections between real life situations or natural phenomenon and the processes of factoring and multiplying polynomials. We will accomplish this by finding analogies in our lives with the two concepts. Please answer the following questions. We will start by using this form in class, then you will develop your final responses at home. Let you imagination roam freely. I have no prior ideas about what form your response will take. Please type your final responses.

How are multiplying and factoring polynomial opposites? Give your explanation in English without using math symbols. Be as complete as you can in your description.

_____

_____

_____

Can you find a situation in nature or your own life activities that is analogous to factoring and multiplying polynomials? Again describe your activity using complete sentences.

_____

_____

_____

Student Responses

Student #1

Multiplying polynomials is like adding them or combining them together. Factoring is breaking them down into their basic parts.

I do upholstering and factoring is like ripping the piece of furniture down, taking off the fabric padding, and in some cases taking apart the frame. Factoring is the same because you are breaking the polynomial into its basic parts. Multiplying polynomials on the other hand is like upholstering in that you are putting the piece of furniture together by adding the spring, padding, and fabric together and when you multiply you combine parts of the polynomial which have like terms after you multiply.

Student #2

Simply put when multiplying polynomials the result is one flat, complete equation whereas in factoring you are breaking the expression down into its' simplest form with its components visible.

It's a strange game fate plays with us.

The joyous experiences we have, and the heart rendering times.

The parents who raised us out of blood or love or the combination.

The neighborhood we grew up in, rural or urban.

People we new taken away from us through physical move or death.

All of these things make us the person we are today, albeit with room for improvement. The formula is fairly simple: Loved ones + experiences + our surroundings. With different people and situations changing with reasonable frequencies though the basic formula stays the same.

Though I've lost other friends and family through death or change of address I don't think I quite appreciated this formula in the truest sense until the death of my father. Actually, more accurately this year. My father died a little over two years ago. The first year was a chaotic nightmare of anger, pain, and resentment. No one could have told me I'd be where I am now. This last year I've started pulling it all together. Accepting now that he's gone physically, I realize this doesn't mean he disappeared altogether. In my actions and my thoughts he'll be around.

So are all the friends we've had and lost. It's not the present we are made of. It's all the factors of our years combined that make us and will bring us to the future. They will hold us up in harder times to come. Nothing ever leaves com-

pletely, it is always there in the formula for our lives. We just
need to recognize the factors to understand how we are made
up.

Student #3

Last evening I took a walk on the beach. It was glori-
ous! The air temperature was perfect, soft and balmy; the tide
was receding, leaving firm wet sand to walk upon. In contrast
to the air, the sand felt like cool velvet. The sun was a bright
orange sphere slowly sinking into the sea. My senses were
being filled on all levels. The air was fresh with pockets of
that marshy seaweed scent that can only be found at low tide.
I always refer to it as the "Oceans Musk."

As I walked I began to think about this summer, people
in my life and MATH?! I began to think about families and
relationships and how the factoring of polynomials is much
like our inter-connections with one another. The original expression and how all the numbers and exponents that come
together to make that polynomial will always remain part of
the original, even when they have been factored out and the
original is reduced to it's simplest form. Each number has a
purpose and reason for being part of the whole.

I though of families. Couples come together multiplying. Children are part of the "family expression." They stay
for a time, are factored out as they grow into adulthood, but
they never are totally removed from the original "family polynomial." Having been factored this allows their "number" to
stand separately, or to join other members and multiply forming a new polynomial–but never leaving touch with the original expression from which it came.

Divorce being similar in that we may factor ourselves
out- but are never totally free of that expression. We separate
from it, but it's influences will color our next expression or
polynomial.

The Diary of a Student or Writing a Course Journal

Description

Writing a course journal may be considered analogous to writing a personal diary, with the main difference being that the journal will be shared with someone else whereas a diary is private. Writing a course journal is an important way to help students deal with affective issues regarding the course. Included in the journal are descriptions of student's approaches to dealing with course content and procedures, including emotional responses to class activities, peers, and the instructor, problems faced in completing course requirements, or specific questions regarding course materials or concepts, to name a few possibilities. Writing may span a wide spectrum from being deeply personal to highly technical. It may serve to help students clarify difficult concepts or articulate where their confusion lies. It opens up a variety of avenues for communication between student and teacher or between students. People often find it easier to write about their problems or negative reactions than verbalize their thoughts. This exercise is intended to help students confront and address issues they are dealing with concerning the course.

Students are asked to make journal entries at least three times a week corresponding to the three class meetings when this schedule is used. More entries are encouraged. Students may write about their understanding of concepts developed in class, problems with homework, their response to class procedures or activities and their performance on tests, quizzes or other graded exercises. Students are asked to write in narrative format and provide as much detail as is necessary for the instructor to be able to fully understand the student's concern or observation about an aspect of the course.

In response to the student's comments the instructor has a number of options. The first is to write back to the student in their journal or as a separate document. Students are generally impressed when a teacher takes the time to address their concern by responding in writing. Next the teacher might elect to speak to the student during class, informally or outside of class. Student conferences, based upon journal writing, are a good way to make contact during the semester. Students may be in need of tutoring or direction as indicated by their journal entries. Students may be referred to additional resources for outside help or counseling. An issue raised by an individual may be brought to the attention of the whole class in order to determine if there is

widespread concern among class members about the issue. This can be followed by whole class brainstorming to deal with a particular problem. This give and take interaction occurs throughout the semester through the instructor's periodic collection and review of the journals. It is quite surprising how candid students become as they develop a familiarity with journal writing and witness the benefits to themselves, the instructor and the class as a whole.

Purposes

1. To encourage students to deal with affective issues they are facing regarding their performance in the course and the operation of the course.

2. To create a mechanism for an extended, semester long, writing effort by students which focuses on their role and interaction in the class.

3. To open various lines of communication between student and teacher or between students if the journals are shared within student groups.

4. To help students become better writers through non-graded personal writing.

5. To help students focus on specific course concepts in order

to have them clarify their understanding of those concepts or articulate their lack of understanding.

Alternate Uses

1. Teachers may ask students to address specific questions they have regarding student reactions to course concepts of procedures. This may be done as part of a journal entry or as the entire focus of that days entry

2. Students may be asked to include other forms of writing in the journal, such as a one minute paper, letter to a friend, a poem, etc.

3. Students might be asked to write up their version of a lesson plan for a particular topic, including class activities and an outline of class notes.

Implications/Activities for Collaborative Learning Opportunities

1. Journal writing is generally intended to be an individual student activity since it is based upon personal reflections. However, pairs or groups may be asked to share their journals with each other with the idea of addressing student problems with course content. Students may be able to help each other with personal problems but this approach must be handled carefully by the instructor, perhaps screening personal issues before encouraging groups to deal with them.

2. Groups may be asked to deal with problems identified by individuals with class procedures or activities through brainstorming activities, the results of which are presented to the whole class.

ALGEBRA JOURNAL DESCRIPTION AND FORMAT

We will be keeping a math journal in this class in order to help us keep track of what we are doing and to have a document which we can use for studying for tests and the final exam.

The journal will consist of two parts:

The first part is a written summary of each module using English. The English should be in your own words not a duplication of the text. This section may be used to write out questions you have regarding the material. Bring your journal to class so that you may have your questions answered.

The second part will consist of examples that you make up or take from the book. The page can be arranged vertically or horizontally. Divide each page in half and use one portion for your English description and one half for examples of worked out problems.

I would like to see a reasonably detailed summary which can be used for later review.

The journal will be collected prior to each test and returned after the test. The journal will not be graded, however if you are borderline in a grade a good journal will increase your grade to the next highest level. We are using a plus and minus grade system so a good journal could make a difference as well as help you learn algebra.

In addition to the technical analysis the journal may be used for writing your observations about the material, the class, instructional procedures, how you are doing or what ever else you feel is appropriate to communicate to me. I will write back to you in the journal.

5-CONTENT ENHANCING

Writing about course content enhances students' critical thinking skills through the process of formulating and editing responses to directed questions. The following assignments are oriented toward mathematics classes in general but may be easily adapted to any course content. When students are asked to explain a procedure or develop a training document they must review their own procedures and articulate them in an understandable manner. If students cannot write about the concepts then it is likely that they do not have enough of an understanding of that concept. Writing assignments call the students' attention to such deficiencies and encourage them to edit their writing after restudying the material.

A- Math is with us every day.

B- Math is with us all day.

C- How did you get here? What sequence of events lead you to this course?

D- Write your own textbook section.

E- Becoming an author–Write a short story about how the quadratic equation came to be.

F- Finding examples of math in the media.

G- Draw your very own graph.

H- Solving the mystery of word problems using the two column format plus alternate uses.

I- Engaging partners in a critical thinking exchange of ideas– Write and swap.

J- Vocabulary building through a multi step writing process.

K- Developing comprehension skills by combining writing with collaborative learning activities.

L- Fables–A cooperative exercise.

MATH IS WITH US EVERY DAY

Description

"Why do I need this course?," "What will I ever use this for?" are the eternal questions asked by students taking courses which are not directly related to their majors or by students who have been placed in courses, contrary to their desires, to meet prerequisites, usually based upon an assessment test or evaluation. These types of questions reflect the students negativity rather than being inquisitive and most answers offered by the professor are met with skepticism or outright denial. I have virtually given up trying to convince students of the value of algebra other than to explain how math has helped me think quickly and logically in difficult or problematic situations.

I have not, however, given up trying to answer their questions, I have simply turned the tables on the students with a case specific exercise which asks students to keep a log or journal of at least one activity they engage in during the day which requires them to use math. It should not be the same activity each day. This exercise is carried out over two weeks yielding 14 entries.

Initially the activities the students record use basic math principles. Over time they begin to recognize and record more complex math relationships in their lives. This exercise is followed by one in which they are asked to keep a record of all math activities used during a full day, repeated over three days. By the end of exercise most students come to the realization that they do indeed use math concepts frequently in their daily lives but in a more subtle form than they expected. They begin to accept the idea that while they may not see a direct use of the content covered in class they can see how they use the concepts to think more clearly and effectively.

This exercise can be adapted to other subjects by replacing the topic of math with any other content presentation. While course content, in the form of information, is important, critical thinking skills are also an important element of any class. When students observe how course content is used in their lives they are more likely to see the relevance of courses not directly related to their major field of study.

Purposes

1. To engage students in identifying the value of a class for real life situations.

2. To begin a process of answering the eternal question "Why do I need this course?"

3. To encourage students to make connections between the analysis of a question or problem, writing, and mathematics.

4. To help personalize a course's content, which is normally considered mechanical, by encouraging students to find examples which relate to their life situations.

Alternate Uses

1. Substitute other topics such as where do you see psychology (history, literature, business) concepts used in your life each day.

2. Have students observe other people using math and keep a log of their observations.

3. Ask students to have someone observe them to identify where they use math during the day.

Implications/Applications for Collaborative Learning Opportunities

1. Students share their logs in pairs or larger groups.

2. Groups list and categorize the math operations or concepts used by their members and report to the whole class.

3. Groups contribute to a master list of math activities developed by the whole class in a brainstorming session, followed by activity #2 above.

WRITING ASSIGNMENT- MATH IS WITH US EVERY DAY

I would like you to make a log entry each day for two weeks which describes at least one activity you complete during the day which requires you to use math. Any math operation can be used including arithmetic, algebra, statistics, etc. I want you to describe a different activity each day. You may also add any personal observations or comments you wish to the log about your reactions to doing the math or writing the log.

Write in full sentence form using a paragraph structure for each activity. Weekends are included. You will complete seven paragraphs per week over the two weeks. I calculate that you will hand in 14 log entries over the course of this assignment. That calculation could be used for my first log entry were I to keep a mathematics activity log.

The purpose of this exercise is to help you answer YOUR questions about why you need this course and how algebra applies to your everyday living experiences. As you get comfortable with looking for math activities each day you may log in more that one activity. It is my hope and expectation that by the end of this exercise you will begin to see connections between math concepts and real life problem solving, and perhaps you will see a direct relation between the formulas we are using and life situations. Below are sample log entries from previous student math logs.

Sample log entries

2/9— In Concepts of Biology today we utilized the Chi-Square statistics method to measure differences for random chance in a data sampling. The basic equation to find the level of random chance is $X*2 =(observation-expected)*2/expected$, for each category within the sample. The result was measured against approximate standard measurements according to the number of categories in a sample (degree of freedom) and percentage rate that corresponds to the measurement. This is a statistical method that assists one in developing and testing scientific hypotheses and proving the accuracy of the sampling data.

2/10— I paid my Visa bill today. The minimum I had to pay was $10 but I decided to pay $50 to bring my balance down so that I would have to pay less interest later. My balance was $292. I paid $50. Now my balance was $292-50=$242. I am wondering if it is likely to stay at $242? Only if I resist the temptation to shop till I drop

Student responses

Feb. 20- I stopped at the cafeteria to buy a can of juice. The juice cost $.55. I gave the lady a $1.00 and she gave me $.45 back.

Feb. 21- My son stayed overnight at my mother-in-laws lst night. I had to figure out what time I would pick him up today because he had to be home by 4:30 for hockey practice.

Feb. 22- I stopped for gas this morning. I put $5.00 in the tank. I then stopped for gas on the way home and had the attendant put $15.00 in the tank. I decided to stop a second time because it is cheaper at the station I went to the second time.

Feb. 23- I did my math homework this afternoon. It took me about 20 minutes.

Feb. 24- I spoke to my husband on the phone. He went to Springfield for a hockey tournament with my son. We were figuring out what time I could expect him home. It all depended on whether my son would be playing an extra game.

Feb. 25- Today I balanced my checkbook. I was right on the money. I paid my bills.

Feb. 26- I went grocery shopping and paid for my groceries with a check. I also went to the bank and withdrew money from my savings account to put into my checking account.

Feb. 27- This morning when I got up for school there was snow on the ground and it was still snowing. I had to recalculate my times so I would get to school on time. I had to leave ten minutes earlier.

Feb. 28- I picked up my husbands check from work and went to the bank and deposited it all into my checking account. I had to add this amount to my check book also.

Mar. 1- I stopped for gas and put $5.00 in the tank on my way to school, The gas is $1.39 per gallon. I again stopped for gas on my way home and put $15.00 in the tank. I paid $1.35 per gallon this time. I estimated that I saved about $.55 the second time.

Mar. 2- My son and I had to be in Hyannis at 7:30 a.m. for a hockey game. I had to figure out what time we had to be up and what time we had to leave to cover the 35 mile trip. Part of the trip is highway driving and part is neighborhood.

Mar. 3- My youngest son is sick. I had to regulate his Tylenol dosage for every four hours. I also had to regulate his Amoxicillan so that he would get in three doses for today. His first dose was at 2:30 p.m. He received doses at 6:30 and 10:30 p.m.

Mar. 4- I could sleep a little later this morning because I only had myself to get ready for school. My crew was staying home sick today. I figured that I did not have to get out of bed until 6:30 a.m. That gave me an extra hour to lay around.

Mar. 5- My oldest son is sick today. I had to figure out his doses of medication. He had his first dose at 5:30 a.m. He could have doses every 4 hours so he had them at 9:30, 1:30 and 5:30.

Mar 6.- Today was clean the garage day. I compiled all the returnable bottles. I figured out that I had $6.75 worth of bottles.

Mar. 7- I am really bearing my soul to you because I am running out of things that relate to math. I have started Weight Watchers today. I was allowed to have 3/4 oz. of cold cereal. I did not have a scale to weigh out my cereal so I called my sister who is a math teacher. She told me that 3/4 oz is 9/16 of a cup so how much would 3/4 oz be? I figured that it is a little more than half a cup. I will definitely lose weight if that is all I can eat!

Mar 8.- My husband and I are refinancing our house. We would like to get a 15 year mortgage. We sat down and figured out how much our payments would be at a rate of 9-1/8%. It should increase our payments about $100 per month. He did refinance us at 9-1/8% on a by-weekly schedule so we will pay our mortgage twice a month and have it paid off in 20 years.

MATH IS WITH US ALL DAY

Description

When you get up in the morning and look at the clock one of your first thought is probably "How much time do I have to get up, get dressed, eat, do what ever else I need to do, and get to school or work on time?" Your mind starts functioning very mathematically, without your conscious approval. Yet so many students are under the impression that math has very little to do with their lives. This exercise, when combined with exercise #13–Finding math every day–completely dispels this idea and goes a long way toward providing a rationale for studying math and thus helps to motivate students in classes where anxiety and complacency runs high.

The exercise is completed over three days. Students record all the activities they are involved in throughout the day which involve using math in any form including arithmetic, algebra or geometry. Many of the activities students report on involve basic math operations such as making change, figuring recipes or mileage calculations.

When the students begin to link the apparently independent activities together in a chain of life experiences they start to make associations with the math concepts they are studying. For example, the order of operation agreement in math specifies the order in which numerical operations must be carried out. When one goes to work or school a series of activities must be completed in a given order to be successful and arrive on time. Problem solving in general requires an orderly approach based upon a set of rules or physical principles. When taken out of order the problem is often exacerbated.

A second benefit of this exercise is realized when students write their observations in English. Their critical thinking skills are enhanced and reinforced. An important connection id developed between organizing one's thoughts and writing them in a coherent paper and concepts developed through mathematics. Students often separate the two areas according to content, thus missing the importance of reading, writing and mathematics.

Purposes

1. To stimulate students critical thinking and observation skills.

2. To emphasize the importance of writing and reading to understanding mathematical concepts.

3. To make real life connections with mathematical concepts and student experiences. This is especially important for older students.

4. To encourage the students to answer the their questions regarding the need to study math.

Alternate Uses

1. While this exercise was developed for math classes, other content areas may be substituted.

2. Students make arrangements to observe a group member during a school day or longer.

3. Include student observations in a portfolio or journal.

4. Students undertake a more extensive analysis of their math activities and relate specific math rules or concepts to their actions.

Implications/applications for collaborative learning opportunities

1. Pairs share their logs and discuss each others activities as they relate to math concepts.

2. Groups discuss their logs and develop a listing of activities grouped with math concepts.

3. Whole class brainstorming may be used to combine group logs into a master list relating real life activities and math concepts.

4. Pairs or larger groups write and essay on the importance of math in our daily lives.

WRITING ASSIGNMENT- MATH IS WITH US ALL DAY

We are going to repeat the previous exercise (#13 Math is with us Everyday) with a slight variation. I would like you to keep a log of math activities you use throughout an entire day. Record each activity you carryout during a day which involves any use of math. Generally try to use single sentences instead of paragraphs unless additional information is necessary to clarify your activity. Please use three different days. use this sheet as a guide or use a separate sheet for each day if you need more room. Do not limit yourself to the number activities listed.

Day #1- date _____

1. _____
2. _____
3. _____
4. _____
5. _____

Day #2-date _____

1. _____
2. _____
3. _____
4. _____
5. _____

Day #3- date _____

1. _____
2. _____
3. _____
4. _____
5. _____

Student responses

Day #1- Monday, July 1

1. I ate at Burger King and the meal cost $3.17. I gave them $5.00 and got $1.83 back.

2. I went to the gym to pay my membership fee for July and had to subtract $40 from my balance to balance my checkbook.

3. The treadmill at the gym indicated that I used up 680 calories in 45 minutes of fast walking. I need to find out how to convert that to pounds or ice cream Sundaes.

4. I paid my car insurance and had to "niggle" money from another account so that my check wouldn't bounce.

Day #2- Tuesday, July 2

1. I took my brother to the registry and had to find out how much it would cost to get his permit and license. I had to add the two to get the total cost. Also we calculated how long it would be before he was able to drive by himself.

2. Went to the mall and bought some sneakers. They cost $22.99 and I had $30. I had to add the change from the $30 to the $22.99 to check the change.

3. Washed the rug today. I had to add fifteen minutes to 5 o'clock to know when to vacuum the wash off.

Day Three- Wednesday- July 3

1. I worked on math homework for 2 1/2 hours, part of my everyday life this summer.

2. I counted the number of hours we will spend in class this summer. At three hours times two days per week for seven weeks the total will be 42 hours.

3. I counted the number of hours I worked this week and divided that number into my total tips to find out how much I made per hour. Not an awful lot!

4. I figured that if I did math homework four days a week for the next seven weeks I would spend 70 hours on math in addition to the 42 class hours for a total of 112 hours. That better get me through algebra!

HOW DID YOU GET HERE– WHAT SEQUENCE OF EVENTS LEAD YOU TO THIS COURSE?

Description

Students rarely make connections between their life situations and course content or concepts learned in courses, especially algebra based classes. One of the primary benefits of studying algebra is that students develop an orderly, analytical approach to problem solving based upon a series of rules and operations. A topic such as following orders of operations appears to be primarily a mechanical application of a set of rules, yet in reality it involves making a series of decisions based upon options available. As we act throughout the day to accomplish a set of goals we make very similar mathematical decisions. We can chose an efficient process to complete our activities or we can follow a series of unrelated activities which may involve many repetitions, such as going to the store several times for individual items versus making one trip to obtain all the items one needs for the day or week. This exercise will help students make a connection between the concept of orderly operations and their daily activities by asking them to record all the activities they completed and decisions they made in order to sign up for and attend the class.

As you will see from the student response upon her completion of the assignment that she has a feeling of uncertainty about the "correctness" of his approach, followed by a sense of clarity as she finally sees the connection between her writing and mathematics concepts. Her response represents a major benefit of personal writing in math. Students are encouraged to reflect upon their work and alter their perceptions of themselves in relation to course content. The process of writing often causes students to re-evaluate their views and approaches to thinking about and doing math as well as how they approach life situations.

Purposes

1. To help students make connections between math concepts and a significant real life activity.

2. To use writing to encourage students to make a personal connection with the course.

3. To cause students to reflect upon how they make decisions in their daily lives.

4. To encourage students to re-evaluate their decision making procedures in light of new information provided during the course.

5. To emphasize the value of WAC in math as a tool for the analysis of problem solutions.

6. To open a line of communication between the student and teacher based upon personal student writing.

Alternate Uses

1. Students may be asked for a more detailed analysis of each decision made during the entire process in order to determine what "rules" were used in making decisions.

2. Students may be asked to analyze what influenced or determined their decisions as they worked through the process of signing up for the course.

3. Students may be asked to try to relate their decisions to content from other courses, such as psychology, business or accounting, etc., to see how their decisions were influenced by concepts covered in these courses.

Implications/Applications for Collaborative Learning Opportunities

1. Using pairs have each student read their analysis to their partner. Their task is to determine if each partner's procedure follows a rational or reasonable order of operations.

2. Pairs, working together, write a short analysis of how their activities resemble orders of operations. This report will be read to the whole class in a plenary session.

3. Pairs or larger groups may be asked to devise a set of rules or orders of operations which would optimize the process of registering for a class.

4. Groups write a synopsis on how this exercise resembles using the orders of operations concepts.

HOW DID YOU GET HERE???

How did you arrive in this class? I would like you to think about the steps you followed and decisions you made which lead you to enroll in this class. Think back to the very beginning of the process and write out the steps you accomplished up to the point in time when you attended the first class.

List the steps, actions or decisions you made in chronological order from the moment you started thinking about taking a course. For example, what started you thinking about taking any course at all? Did you talk to someone about the decision to obtain advice or just go out a get a school catalogue? Explain each step using complete sentences. You may number each step if it helps you keep track of what you did. Try not to leave anything out even though it may seem obvious or simplistic. Please type your analysis.

As you work your way through this assignment I would like you to think about what relation it has to specific concepts we are studying in mathematics. Some questions I would like you to consider are:

1. Does decision making in real life have any relation to mathematical concepts?

2. Can the use of math concepts improve your approach to solving problems in real life?

3. Can you think of specific examples of math concepts, not necessarily specific operations but general concepts, which you have applied during the process described above?

Student response

How did Pat get into a summer algebra class? The following are the steps I took to arrive in this class:

1. I graduated from high school in 1978, then attended Southern Connecticut University for two years.

2. At the end of my second year I dropped out of school.

3. During the next few years I worked as a waitress, bartender and bank teller.

4. At this time I began to think about returning to school. I qualified for Massachusetts Rehabilitation Assistance and took a few courses while working as a circulation manager for the local newspaper.

5. I did not have clear career goals and was busy building a home, getting married and having two children. I had a hard time getting motivated about school.

6. In March, right before my second child was born, I shut down Curtain Climbers Inc., my home daycare business. At this point I began thinking seriously about returning to school full time in September.

7. I have had mostly positive work experiences, but couldn't get a job I could really enjoy, work to my potential and get paid enough to live on without a college degree. With that in mind I still was having a hard time getting motivated for school. My life seemed to demand more than I already had to give.

8. This past February I contacted and attended a meeting at the Women In Transition program at Cape Cod Community College.

9. At this time my marriage hit a severe crisis and the possibility of being a single parent of two small children became a reality. Realizing that I need to be able to support myself and two small children and the fear of being homeless on welfare gave me the biggest shot of motivation I could have possibly needed.

10. I filled out and mailed my school application and financial aid form.

11. Next I contacted Frank in the counseling center for an appointment to evaluate my transfer credits.

12. After our meeting, on the Wednesday before this class started, I found out I only needed 20 credits to graduate, but I needed to have at least pre-calculus.

13. At this point I was planning to attend the University of Massachusetts at Dartmouth after Cape Cod but in order for me to get the math requirement in and still finish the associates degree by next June I would need Algebra this summer.

14. I contacted Bruce at Mass. rehab. and met with him on Thursday before class started and convinced him to let me get into this class. He was very reluctant because there was a lot of paper

work to be done and he was getting ready to go on vacation.

15. Now I needed to make daycare arrangements. I found a daycare center for Wednesdays and my mother volunteered for Mondays.

16. Monday morning before class I went to the bookstore, there were no books.

17. I was very nervous by the time I got to the first class and then found out there had been an assignment already given. Being very determined I knew things would work out somehow.

18. I knew math classes require a lot of homework but I was not prepared to do writing assignments. That is my most fearful part of being in school next to having to do public speaking or a presentation.

19. Fortunately Mr. Panitz, my instructor, had a book for me. I spent every spare minute from the first to the second class in it, reviewing the first four chapters.

20. I am feeling more confident now because I am managing to do the homework and I did well on the two mastery tests we have had.

21. I am uncomfortable about this assignment because I don't know if I did it right.

This process is like solving equations or word problems because each step simplifies the problem and brings you closer to the goal. Each step breaks the problem down and simplifies it until the solution is reached. First one big problem is formulated then it is broken down into many small problems which can be more easily solved to bring you to the solution.

Write Your Own Textbook Section

Description

Students use a variety of sources to obtain information on course content necessary for their understanding of concepts and facts. The teacher serves as a primary source and organizer of information. The textbook serves as the majority source of factual information and supplemental reading or audiovisual materials provide secondary sources of information. Students generally accept the materials presented to them as coming from expert sources. Rarely do they question the content or organization of texts or course materials or the reasoning which lies behind those materials. This exercise requires students to consider how a difficult subject might be presented based upon their own perspectives by asking them to write a section of a textbook chapter. The sample provided below asks students to write a section which explains how to solve word problems. This is an area of general concern for most students who find the concept of translating English into algebraic equations especially difficult.

The process of writing a section of a textbook requires a high degree of critical thinking, A thorough understanding of the material under study is needed as well as good organization skills. Students need to be able to understand the nature of the material as well as be able to complete chapter problems and questions plus they need to restate the process in their own words in such a way as to be understandable to their peers. This exercise goes well beyond the usual student process of reading the material, completing practice questions and then reproducing the facts or process on an exam.

In effect this exercise calls upon students to become teachers and authors for a brief time as they organize the content by presenting a lesson in written form. It is when we attempt to teach someone else a concept that we really learn that concept. Writing, especially, highlights whether we know how to explain an idea or process because the end product is used by others. The process of writing a book section allows one to edit our work, change our approaches and even modify our own thoughts about the subject under investigation. Students are called upon to use their imagination to explain concepts. The writing process often helps them clarify difficult concepts by writing about those concepts in terms they and their peers can relate to. Students by being closer to their peers often find ways of explaining course material more clearly than the professor whose vocabulary and intellectual level is quite different from the students.

Purposes

1. To provide a mechanism for student exploration of difficult concepts in depth.

2. To help students construct their own process for solving story problems.

3. To expose students to the process of writing explanatory "text" materials.

Alternate Uses

1. Students edit existing book chapters or sections to reflect their personal experiences, adding their own examples, vocabulary and order of presentation.

2. Students act as book reviewers or critics and analyze chapter sections.

Implications/Activities for Collaborative Learning Opportunities

1. Student teams work together to develop chapter sections in a jigsaw exercise where
each team develops a different section of the chapter, becoming experts on that material and teaching it to the other teams.

2. Students work in teams to develop the entire chapter.

Write Your Own Textbook Chapter Section

HOW TO SOLVE WORD PROBLEMS

Many students find mathematics textbooks hard to read because of the technical nature of the vocabulary and presentation format. I would like you to try your hand at writing a section of a textbook on the topic of solving word problems. Based upon your current knowledge and any other resources which might be available to you develop a textbook chapter or section which explains the process/procedure for solving word problems.

Be as original as you like and use what ever illustrations or examples you feel would be helpful to a beginner trying to learn how to set up and solve word problems. Especially consider your own approach and reactions to learning word problems and use your hindsight to prepare materials which will help your fellow students.

By original I mean you may use interesting examples, tell a story, write a poem etc. Use what ever strategy you think will get your readers attention and make a strong impression on them plus help them remember your suggested process.

Please type your text section. You may hand write equations if your word processor does not include that function, but the text should be typed.

Student response

Strategy for Solving Word problems

Ask a student to solve a word problem and you will probably get a bunch of moans. They often seem much more difficult than they really are. All they are, are a bunch of words and once you know how to decipher them, they are all pretty basic. You just need to translate them into an equation and then solve.

I would first determine what kind of problem it is. Certain word problems have specific formulas to follow. There are discount problems ($S=R-rR$), markup problems ($S=C+rC$), investment problems (I=Prt), mixture problems (V=AC), uniform m option problems (d=rt), or geometry problems (P=2L + 2W). Also, it is necessary to translate certain English words into a mathematical expression. For instance, the word "is" means equal to. "Less than" or "difference" means subtraction. "The product of" means multiplication or "quotient" means division. There are many other phrases but they are similar in meaning.

Once you have determined which formula you will need to know, the next step is to determine what it is the word problem wants to know. What is it asking? For example, in a discount problem you may be asked to find the discount amount or discount rate or discount time. Next take the information you do know and plug it into the equation. Discount problems have the formula S+R-rR. In a discount problem where they ask you to find the sale price of a pair of shoes, they tell you that they regularly sell for $55 and are on sale for 25% off. Well, they are asking for "S" in the formula. They tell you "R" is $55, the regular selling price, and "r" is 25%, the discount rate. So you now have this: S=55 - 0.25(55). The 25% becomes 0.25 because you have translated the number from a percent to a decimal in order to multiply. When you do the math you get S= $41.25. Therefore, the sale price of a pair of shoes is $41.25.

In other problems you can benefit from making a chart and filling in the information you know. In doing this, sometimes you can derive your own information from just a little bit of information they have given you. With this information and the information they gave you one can solve such problems as investment, mixture, and uniform motion.

For example, in an investment problem, they may give you the total amount invested in two accounts and want to know how much was invested in each account. You have to assign account #1 a variable, say X. Then you know that account #2 is the total money invested minus the first account which is X. This problem does not state this, it is something you must deduce on your own using common sense. It helps to make a chart.

	P*	R	=	I
acct. #1	X			
acct. #2	24000- X			
total	24000			

Next the problem gives you the simple interest rate of each account. Account #1 is 4%, account #2 is 9% and the total interest earned is 7%. Fill in the chart with this information.

	P*	R	=	I
acct. #1	X	0.04		
acct. #2	24000- X	0.09		
total	24000	0.07		

Next you figure out that PR=I. Therefore in account #1 the "I" is 0.04X, in account #2 it is 0.09(24,000 -X) and in the total it is 0.07(24,000). Complete the rest of the chart.

	P*	R	=	I
acct. #1	X	0.04		0.04X
acct. #2	24000- X	0.09		0.09(24,000 -X)
total	24000	0.07		0.07(24,000)

Now, what ever interest "I" in account #1 plus #2 is equal to the total interest. You are not told this information in so many words, but it is something you may figure out from the information given and what you already know about how saving accounts work. You can now make an equation: 0.04X + 0.09(24,000 - X) = 0.07(24,000). Once the math is done you find X = $9600.

The problem wants to know how much is invested in each account. To find out the amount in the second account you plug 9600 into account number 2 and get 24,000 - 9600 = 14,400. Therefore $9600 was invested in account #1 and $14,400 was invested in account #2. The total is 24,000 which we already knew so this checks out the answer.

You would use the same chart for rate and mixture problems using their respective formulas at the top of the chart. Once you get used to solving word problems they all seem alike even though they ask you for different information. It is just a matter of plucking out just the information you need. The more you do the problems the more familiar they get and they actually begin to seem easy.

Becoming an author–Write a short story about how the quadratic formula came to be

Description

Story telling has been a favorite form of communication since the beginning of recorded existence when cave people used charcoal to draw pictures on cave walls. This exercise takes us well beyond those days and into the future of computer word processing and graphics. The use of a short story to highlight a particular course concept is especially compelling as it allows the author to explore her/his imagination in developing an explanation of the concept based upon their own personal experiences.

When students write a short story they use all the critical thinking elements of essay writing including brainstorming, organization of materials, writing ,editing and rewriting etc. In addition the student must integrate course content into the thought process in a clear and concise manner. Concepts and procedures must be thoroughly understood before one can describe them in a coherent fashion. This exercise harnesses the energy and skill potential of students who like to write but do not feel competent in courses such as mathematics and science or who do not make connections with the content of non-writing courses. This is especially true in math courses where abstract symbolism is hard for many students to relate to.

An additional benefit occurs from this exercise when students describe or use a concept in such a way as to clarify it for their peers. Students are often able to articulate the reasons behind difficult concepts or involved procedures using vocabulary and examples their fellow students can relate to effectively.

Purposes

1. To help students understand involved concepts or extended procedures by using a process which stimulates their imagination.

2. To help students make connections between course concepts and real life, fictional or hypothetical situations.

3. To stimulate student interest in course material through a fun writing exercise.

4. To encourage students to make connections between academic subjects through writing.

Alternate Uses

1. Students may use alternate forms of writing such as poetry, writing a news article from a reporters perspective, preparing a short documentary, op-ed article or letter to the editor, etc.

2. Students may be involved in a contest for best short story as judged by their peers. Criteria for judging may be established by the class or the instructor.

3. A one act play might be produced by groups or the whole class to illustrate course content.

Implications/Applications for Collaborative Learning Activities

1. Individuals read their stories to their groups first followed by editing and rewriting and then reading to the whole class. This creates an opportunity for repeating a review of a concept from several students' perspectives.

2. Pair or group editing of each students work followed by a rewrite.

3. Enactment of a play by groups or the whole class.

4. Preparation of a book of short stories with each group contributing their members stories.

WRITING A PULITZER PRIZE WINNING SHORT STORY

HOW DID THE QUADRATIC FORMULA COME TO BE?

In order to help you understand the nature of the derivation of generalized formulas in mathematics I would like you to analyze the derivation of the quadratic formula. We will use different tactic in this assignment than using pure mathematics. I would like you to write a short story which describes how the quadratic formula came to be. Let your imagination roam freely as you explain each separate operation, starting with the general form of the quadratic equation, $aX^2 + bX + C = 0$ and arriving at the quadratic formula.

The purpose of this exercise is to help you understand how mathematicians think and work by your working through the formal derivation of the quadratic formula. The actual derivation is very mechanical. This exercise is intended to add some spice to the process and hopefully help you remember the process by having you make up a story in your own words based upon your own experiences.

Use your imagination to its fullest. You may write a fiction or nonfiction story, biography or autobiography, character description or other form as you see fit. Try to write your story with your fellow students in mind and the question "How will your story help your peers understand the derivation better?"

Student response

Once upon a time there were three constants (A, B, C) and a variable (X). They tried to coexist in the same quadratic equation but couldn't solve their problem.

$$AX + BX + C = 0$$

They decided that a possible solution was to create a new equation by moving the third constant next door and advertise for another constant.

$$AX + BX = -C$$

But trouble arose and the first constant had to be moved to the floor below.

$$1/A(AX) + 1/A(BX) = 1/A(-C)$$
$$X + B/A(X) = -C/A$$

The next plan, in order to complete the square, was to create a new constant (alas, no constants replied to the ad). This was accomplished by dividing the second constant by two and squaring the answer.

$$(1/2*B/A) = B/4A$$

This was such a good idea that the constant's twin decided to move in next door to keep things in balance.

$$X + BX/A + B/4A = B/4A - C/A$$

Now that the constants were done moving about it was time to tidy up. This was done by factoring the left side first.

$$(X + B/2A)^2 = B/4A - C/A$$

Then a single fraction was created on the right side by creating a common denominator.

$$(X + B/2A)^2 = B/4A - (C/A)(4A/4A)$$
$$(X + B/2A) = \sqrt{B/4A - (B^2 - 4AC)/4A}$$

Next a square root was applied to both sides of the equation in accordance with the rules of solving equations.

$$(X + B/2A) = \sqrt{B/4A - (B^2 - 4AC)/4A}$$

Both sides were simplified to make it easier for every-one to see what had happened

$$X - B/2A = \sqrt{(B^2 - 4AC)/2A}$$

Then it happened. The first variable of the first term decided to go it alone and moved the new constant next door.

$$X = -B/2A \sqrt{(B^2 - 4AC)/2A}$$

This infuriated the new constant but ultimately found the new arrangements acceptable and, after combining all their like terms on the right, found it possible to solve the qua-dratic equations that had been so elusive. And that is the story of the quadratic equation

$$X = \frac{-B \sqrt{B^2 - 4AC}}{2A}$$

WAC - EXERCISE #5F

Finding Examples of math in the Media

Description

Print media including newspapers, magazines, journals and other forms provide a rich source of real life, practical examples which illustrate concepts discussed in academic courses. This is especially true of mathematics where writer of all types use math-ematical principles or operations to justify opinions, highlight the theme of a particular article, or justify a conclusion. The business and sports sections or newspapers are perhaps the richest source of math based articles. Even the comics section has many examples of subtle humor based upon the direct use of numbers and math concepts or which use society's anxiety over math in general.

In this exercise students are asked to find three articles, from print media of their choice, which use mathematical principles to make a point. Articles from magazines which represent hobbies or special interests of the students are most appropriate. The use of newspaper stories which deal with a student's personal issue or current topic of interest are also encouraged in order to personalize the analysis. Students provide an overview of the article, a description of exactly how math was used, whether the article changed or reinforced their opinion, especially if based upon the mathematics, and what they concluded about the article. Their analysis is to include an explanation of how math was used to convince the reader that the article's thesis was correct and whether the author succeeded in making his/her point convincingly.

Research is clear, especially with adults, when concepts are formulated or demonstrated by students based upon their personal experiences they are more likely to understand and remember the concepts being studied. This exercise emphasizes this learning strategy by having students find articles which are of interest to them and have real meaning in their lives. It then asks them to build on their prior experiences by critically analyzing each article and its impact upon their views of a particular issue. The purpose behind requesting three articles is to demonstrate the wide application of math in the real world and to encourage students to build upon their analytical and writing skills through successive writing efforts.

Purposes

1. To help students relate their general interest reading to course content, in this case to help answer the question of why one should study math.

2. To encourage students to answer questions about where the course content appears in their daily lives.

3. To make connections between course concepts and other information oriented materials such as newspapers and magazines.

Alternate Uses

1. Students may be asked to find examples of specific course content areas which are used or discussed in print media.

2. Students might be asked to write and article for a newspaper or magazine using concepts developed through the class. This might include a news story, general interest story about hobbies,

travel, entertainment etc., an interview or other activity.

3. Students may be asked to edit or rewrite an article based upon their own opinions or conclusions, using course concepts or other analytical procedures.

Implications/Applications for Collaborative Learning Opportunities:

1. Individuals read these articles to their groups or in pairs followed by their article analysis and receive feedback from group members on their analysis.

2. The teacher may pick an article of general interest to the class and ask pairs of students to review and analyze the article.

3. Along the lines of activity #2, the class might pick an article for additional analysis after individuals read their examples or based upon each group's selection of their favorite article.

WRITING ASSIGNMENT- FINDING EXAMPLES OF MATH IN THE MEDIA

Mathematics is used in some very subtle and some not so subtle ways in their print media which we come in contact with every day. I have provided you with some of my favorite newspaper articles which deal with education and learning issues. I have also presented a number of examples of what I consider practical math problems based upon real life stories and advertisements I have found in print media. Now it is your turn. I would like you to find three articles from newspapers or other print media you read on a regular basis which use math to make a point. Analyze the article and explain how math was used to convince the reader that the thesis of the article was correct.
Your analysis should include:

- A summary of the article.
- What the main point of the article was?
- How math concepts or operations were used in the article?
- Whether the article gave you information which you did not previously have.

- Whether the article changed or reinforced your opinion about the topic .
- Your conclusions about the article.

WAC - EXERCISE #5G

How Do Your Draw A Graph?

Description

Many students develop mathematical procedures by practicing problem exercises in a repetitive, rote manner, without ever thinking about the concepts, structure or rules behind the concepts they are studying. This rote method of learning mathematics has significant limitations. Students frequently complain that they cannot recall the procedure several weeks after they thought they had mastered it. This observation by students is backed up by learning theory which holds that in order to strengthen memory one must practice nonrote ways of studying concepts. Asking students to write about their understanding of concepts is one way to encourage nonrote learning by building students' vocabulary and through editing of their writing. A second way to encourage nonrote learning is to have students share their writing efforts, peer edit each other's work and by asking students to write a common description or procedure by arriving at a consensus approach.

This exercise provides an extended procedure within which students analyze their own processes for drawing graphs, write out these processes as a guide for their peers, share their descriptions and then develop a combined write up based upon input from each partner. The process has at least two nonrote critical thinking components in the writing exercises completed individually and in pairs. Students must think carefully about what each step in the graphing process accomplishes and then communicate this in writing. They then must share this information with a peer and come to a consensus about what elements of each student's process should be included in the final description. The students work out an agreement on vocabulary, order of operations and presentation format.

This information may then be shared with another pair for final peer editing and to determine if each set of procedures is understandable to an outside observer.

Purposes

1. To help students learn how to develop study procedures which will improve their memory of mathematical concepts.

2. To encourage students to think critically about a process which appears to be a rote operation.

3. To help students build their mathematical vocabulary by talking to their peers and negotiating a consensus approach to a mathematical procedure.

4. To provide a social experience within which students clarify their understanding of concepts

Alternate Uses

This exercise may be adapted to any procedure which requires many sequential steps or operations. Whenever students write out a description of a process they must think critically about each step and proper location of each process, versus mechanically carrying out each step in a rote manner.

2. Larger groups can be used to develop a consensus description. Larger groups facilitate the study of group interactions and require more consensus building and negotiation of the appropriate vocabulary needed to explain a particular concept.

3. The final products may be used to help students learn the process better. Often students understand their peers more readily than they do the instructor because they speak the same language which is evolving as they study a subject versus the professor who has an established vocabulary and personal understanding of the concepts under study.

Implications/Applications for Cooperative Learning Opportunities

1. This exercise is intended to be completed using cooperative learning structures. Students first work individually to start the process of learning the concept and procedures and then share their understanding with another student. This is followed by pairs

sharing their work and combining the best of both student's work into one document. The pairs may share their work with a larger group or with the whole class.

2. Groups may be asked to analyze their performance at reaching a consensus document and suggest ways of improving how they work together.

HOW TO DRAW A GRAPH–MY VERY OWN PROCEDURE

You are asked to draw linear graphs of the two equations on the attached sheet.

PART 1-You are to develop a written procedure for drawing a graph of the equation on the left side. Work individually and list every step you take to produce your graph. Leave nothing out even if you consider the step to be very simple or obvious. List the steps numerically 1-100 or how ever many steps you need to complete the graph.

PART 2- Share your description with your partner and compare your procedures. Make a special note of any differences in vocabulary you each use. Then work together to write a unified (consensus) procedure for drawing a graph of the equation on the right side of the attached sheet. Use the back of the paper if necessary.

Procedure for drawing a linear graph- PART 1

1._____

_____

_____

_____

Procedure for drawing a linear graph- PART 2

1._____

_____

_____

_____

Solving the mystery of word problems using the two-column format plus alternate uses for the two-column format

Description

The two-column format is a unique method for relating written explanations to abstract mathematical processes. A problem many people encounter when they study mathematics arises because they learn to memorize procedures without fully understanding the concepts or rules behind the operations. When they are asked to explain their rationale they are at a loss. Having students explain their methods by writing explanations in English as they work through a problem causes them to think critically and reflectively. The process helps students clarify what they know and what they do not understand and often enables them to formulate questions which helps them learn difficult concepts.

In the two-column format the student divides the worksheet into two columns. The left column is used to work out a math problem using a sequential step by step procedure. The right column is used for a written explanation of each step. Several examples of different uses of the two-column format will be presented.

In the first sample assignment students are asked to focus on their thoughts as they attempt to solve a word problem. A significant problem associated with story problems occurs when students become distracted by the story line and their thoughts stray from the problem solution process to the story itself. In the example problem students are asked to relate costs for two different car rental companies. This often elicits students memories of trips or vacations or other occasions where they were involved in renting a car.

When students write out their thoughts exactly as they think them along with their mathematical steps it becomes evident exactly how distracted they can become. Solving math problems, especially word problems, requires a great deal of concentration. Writing helps students focus on the process and increases their ability to concentrate on the problem at hand.

This exercise is intended to be completed during a class followed by a whole class discussion. Students are asked to read their responses verbatim. The level of student distraction during the exercise becomes quite evident after only a few students have read their papers. A class discussion may now be facilitated which focuses on developing work strategies for successfully completing word problems by raising students awareness of their need to concentrate on the problem by rereading the problem statement many times and maintaining a level of patience when they do not come to an immediate solution, to name a few.

Two additional examples of the use of the two-column format are provided. In the first case a sample problem is worked out showing each step in the process. The student analyses each step and writes their explanation of what rule or procedure was used to accomplish that step. The second case is an extension of the first. Here students must solve a similar problem to case one using their own approach, which may model the example provided by the teacher, giving explanations of their steps for each operation they use. These approaches have many possible collaborative opportunities as will be described in more detail below.

Purposes

1. To help students understand why they have special difficulties when solving word problems compared to solving algebraic problems.

2. To emphasize the need for students to raise their level of concentration when solving word problems and avoid distractions created by the story line of word problems.

3. To underscore the critical thinking nature of solving word problems and other types of mathematical problems.

4. To help students determine the depth of their understand-

ing of mathematical procedures by requiring them to explain their procedures and methods.

Alternate Uses

1. The two-column format may be used with any math problem, even single step problems. It is especially helpful in focusing students attention on their understanding of the nature of any problem. An inability to explain what they are doing indicates a fundamental lack of understanding of the concepts being employed.

2. The two-column format may be used during tests to help students focus on the problem solution and to help the instructor determine the depth of the student's understanding of the problem.

3. This procedure may be applied to homework solutions as well as in class work.

Implications/Applications for Collaborative Learning Opportunities

1. After completing a problem individually students may share their papers with their group or partner.

2. Students may be asked to work the problem in pairs by coming to an agreement on what to write about each step.

3. Students working in pairs may be asked to complete alternate steps by writing out their explanations and then explaining their rationale to their partner.

4. The process used in part three can be extended to larger groups by handing the worksheet around the group after each member completes a step in the solution and explains their rationale to the group.

SOLVING EQUATION USING ALGEBRA AND ENGLISH

The following equation is worked out by completing each operation as a separate activity. Explain in English on the right side of the page what was done on each line to work towards solving the equation.

ALGEBRA SOLUTION   ENGLISH EXPLANATION

$5X + 3(2X - 4) = 7(-5X + 1)$ This is the starting equation.

$5X + 6X - 12 = 7(-5X + 1)$

$11X - 12 = -35X + 7$

$46X - 12 = 7$

$46X = 19$

$X = 19/46$

SOLVING EQUATION USING ALGEBRA AND ENGLISH

Solve the following equation by carrying out one operation at a time using the left hand side of the page. Write an explanation in English describing what you did using the right hand side of the page. Use complete sentences. Use the reverse side of the paper if you need more room.

ALGEBRA SOLUTION_____ ENGLISH EXPLANATION

$3(2X - 5)$ $-7(3X -4) = $ $7X + 8$

Engaging partners in a critical thinking exchange of ideas–Write and Swap

Description

How can you help students examine each others interpretation of course content, concepts, or ideas presented in the text? One mechanism involves having students chose a sentence or phrase written in a text passage or presented by the teacher, writing their interpretation or opinion of the material and then asking their partner to comment, also in writing. After each person has completed both the written and comment sections of the worksheet a discussion follows to clarify each others ideas and reactions to the comments. This exercise is most effective using pairs of students, however larger groups can be accommodated.

This exercise has a number of interesting components. First, students chose material which attracts their attention the most within the context of the material being studied. This helps insure student interest and enables students to relate to a particular idea presented in the text. Second, students are asked to provide their own commentary in the form of opinions or analysis. This requires a high degree of critical thinking since students must decide what they feel is important to comment on and then organize their thoughts accordingly. Third, students must read their partner's analysis by first finding the sentence or phrase chosen, putting that phrase into context and then reading the comments of their partner. Fourth, they must formulate a reaction to their partners writing and respond in writing. This process also calls for a high degree of critical thinking and organization. Fifth, students discuss their initial writing and comments. This final activity provides a strong oral component to the exercise in the form of students questioning each other, debating their ideas and opinions, defending their views and attempting to reach an understanding of each other's views and possibly reaching a consensus opinion on the material under study.

This activity is highly student centered since the students chose the material they wish to comment on and then react to each others thoughts. Discussions following the initial writing and exchange of papers is always lively and interesting as students present their opinions and defend them to their peers. Students are surprised and impressed at the diversity of opinion elicited by this exercise and by the fact that they often reach a consensus about the subject matter after they have had a chance to explore each other's perspectives.

The example presented is taken from a history course and focuses on issues involving the civil war. Virtually any content material is adaptable to this format.

Purposes

1. To provide a multiphase writing and oral communication exercise which stimulates several modes of critical thinking.

2. To help personalize course content by asking the students to chose the section of the material they wish to comment on.

3. To provide a mechanism for students to interact through writing, analyzing peer writing and oral communication.

4. To encourage students to share their ideas and opinions about course concepts with their peers and the class as a whole.

5. To encourage students to organize their thoughts in a concise, focused manner by being as specific as possible and by providing a short space to write in.

6. To encourage students to express and defend their opinions regarding course concepts or ideas.

Alternate Uses

1. Students may be asked to edit each others comments for content, grammar, organization and appropriateness to the topic.

2. A rewrite mechanism may be included where students edit and rewrite their comments based upon their discussions with their partners.

3. The initial comments and responses may be read to the whole class for additional discussion in a plenary class session.

---

4. The comments made by students may be used as a basis for further discussions or additional follow up questions.

Implications/Applications for Collaborative Learning Opportunities

1. This exercise is intended to be completed as a collaborative learning activity using pairs of students. The interactions are self explanatory. However, variations may be used by changing the group size.

2. When using groups of three or more a round robin exercise may be employed where students pass their papers to the person on their right for comments. Each member then reads the original writing plus their comments in order to facilitate a group discussion among all three partners. One paper is discussed at a time to avoid confusion.

3. When using groups of three, the extra person may serve as facilitator and help guide the discussion/debate between the other two members as they discuss their writing. In this pattern each member will get to function as a facilitator at least once.

4. If groups of four are used then a number of patterns are available; a round robin exchange of papers similar to number 3 above; a discussion among two members while the other two observe and comment on the discussion after it is completed; discussion by all members after each paper is read to the group.

WRITE AND SWAP EXERCISE

The Civil War (1861-1865)

Pick a sentence or group of sentences and comment on them either by explaining whether you agree or disagree with the author, or whether you have had similar experiences as described in the sentence(s), or in any other way you might relate to what the author is saying. UNDERLINE THE SENTENCES YOU CHOSE TO COMMENT ON. Write your comments in the space provided below and the pass your paper to your partner. Read the sentences your partner underlined, read the analysis and then comment upon their writing. Do you agree or disagree? Explain why.

The South's attack on Fort Sumpter in 1861 started the

Civil War. The Civil War would last for four years and result in the deaths of hundreds of thousands of soldiers. Almost every other American would be affected by the war in some way. The war would even change America itself.

The war came as no surprise to Americans, in the North or in the South. It had been brewing for years in the many angry fights over slavery. Americans did not expect, however, that the war would be so long and costly. They thought it would last only two or three months.

People on both sides responded with energy, even excitement to the call to arms. A young Illinois recruit wrote that "It is worth everything to live in this time." A northern woman wrote, "It seems as if we never were alive till now; never had a country till now." In Washington, D.C., an office worker named Clara Barton took a pistol, put up a target, and fired away.

Use the reverse side of the paper if you need more room.

YOUR COMMENTS

_____

_____

_____

YOUR PARTNERS' COMMENTS

_____

_____

_____

Vocabulary Building Through A Multi step Writing Process

Description

Students who wish to join a specialized academic field face two major obstacles. They lack sufficient knowledge of the vocabulary which governs the academic discipline and they are not capable of conversing with established members of the academic society they wish to join. For example, mathematicians, scientists, social scientists, artists, writers all have their own nomenclature, historically important figures associated with their fields and methodologies for expressing their ideas and findings. The following exercises actively involve students in building a base vocabulary which is discipline specific and in practicing using the new vocabulary to converse with their peers and experts in the field.

The exercise has four different components. First, students are asked to locate a set of vocabulary words within the text. This helps place words in context from the author's (expert's) point of view. Next the words are defined by the students using their own words and examples. They then write a sentence using each word individually. This exercise enables the instructor to determine if the student has an understanding of how each word is used. For an additional study assignment and to reinforce the student's use of each vocabulary word students make up flash cards for each word. These cards may be used as a study guide throughout the semester. In the final assignment students are asked to write a story using all of the words. This aspect of vocabulary development fosters creativity and encourages students to put the words in the context of their own life experiences.

Purposes

1. To provide a mechanism for students to focus on the important vocabulary of an academic specialty.

2. To create an assignment where repetitive use of vocabulary is used to help the students remember the words by using different assignments and approaches in order to avoid the boredom which repetition generates.

3. To help students relate new vocabulary words to the current experiences, thus helping them bridge the gap in vocabulary as they attempt to become members of a new academic society.

4. To encourage creativity and critical thinking in students as they work at entering a new and unfamiliar field of study.

Alternate Uses

1. Students may be included in the initial identification of important words by asking them to list all words which they do not understand in the text. The class then might pick however many words they wish to define which they feel are necessary to understand the material in the chapter.

2. At each phase of the assignment students might be asked to share their results with the class as a whole or with smaller groups.

3. A class definition could be derived with the teacher as facilitator. This should be done prior to having the students use the words in sentences.

4. A class discussion about the nature and importance of building a strong vocabulary in each academic field could be facilitated.

5. Suggestions about how to help students remember the vocabulary words could be solicited from the class as well as ideas for future vocabulary building exercises.

Implications/Applications for Collaborative Learning Opportunities

1. Each individual assignment is tailor made for cooperative learning approaches. Students might work in pairs to complete each section and report their results back to the whole class.

2. Pair reading of the text in order to identify the vocabulary words and place them in context would be ideal for this assignment. In pair reading each partner reads the entire selection first. This is followed by the partners alternating between explaining one paragraph at a time to the other partner and listening to the explanation and questioning the person doing the explaining.

3. A jig-saw structure might be employed where the words are divided up among the members of each base group who then join members from other groups and become experts on the use of their words. They then return to their base groups to teach their group members the new words.

FIND THE MISSING WORDS

1) Two lines in the same plane (or flat surface) that do not (intersect) are parallel lines.

2) Show two (parallel) lines on your desktop, using your models.

3) Imagine that the (plane) or surface of your desktop extends infinitely.

4) Imagine your model lines extending (infinitely) in both directions.

5) Place one model line in any position on your desk. Place another so that it intersects the first, forming a (right angle).

6) How can a line be (perpendicular) to one of your lines but not lie on your desktop?

7) Mark a point R, that is not on PQ. Draw (ray) PR (written PR). Name another (ray) on your diagram.

8) An (acute) angle has a measure less that 90.

9) Perpendicular lines are marked with a square at their (intersection).

10) Name all the (obtuse) angles. Do they all have the same measure?

DEFINE THE FOLLOWING WORDS

YOU MAY USE THE TEXT BUT WRITE THE DEFINITION IN YOUR OWN WORDS

INTERSECT:_____

_____

PARALLEL:_____

_____

PLANE: _____

_____

INFINITELY:_____

_____

RIGHT ANGLE:_____

_____

PERPENDICULAR:_____

_____

RAY:_____

_____

ACUTE:_____

_____

INTERSECTION:_____

_____

OBTUSE:_____

_____

WRITE A SENTENCE USING EACH OF THE MATH VO-
CABULARY WORDS
(INTERECT)_____

_____

(PARALLEL)_____

_____

(PLANE)_____

_____

(INFINITELY)_____

_____

(RIGHT ANGLE)_____

_____

(PERPENDICULAR)_____

_____

(RAY)_____

_____

(ACUTE)_____

_____

(INTERSECTION)_____

_____

(OBTUSE)_____

_____

STUDY AID ASSIGNMENT

WORKING WITH YOUR PARTNER MAKE UP A SET OF "FLASH CARDS" FOR EACH OF THE MATH VOCABULARY WORDS DEFINED PREVIOUSLY. USE 3 X 5 INDEX CARDS.

ON THE FRONT OF THE CARD WRITE THE WORD

ON THE BACK OF THE CARD WRITE THE DEFINITION WHICH WAS AGREED TO BY THE WHOLE CLASS.

ONE PARTNER QUIZZES THE OTHER BY HOLDING UP ONE CARD AT A TIME AND ASKING THEIR PARTNER FOR THE DEFINITION OF THE WORD. WHEN THE FIRST PARTNER IS ABLE TO TELL ALL THE DEFINITIONS CORRECTLY SWITCH CARDS AND QUIZ THE SECOND PARTNER.

THE QUIZ CAN BE REVERSED BY SHOWING YOUR PARTNER THE DEFINITION AND ASKING FOR THE WORD.

WRITE A (MATH) FICTION STORY USING EACH OF THE VOCABULARY WORDS AT LEAST TWICE IN THE STORY.

_____

_____

_____

_____

_____

_____

_____

_____

_____

_____

INTERSECT	PARALLEL
PLANE	INFINITELY
ANGLE	PERPENDICULAR
RAY	ACUTE
INTERSECTION	OBTUSE

Developing Comprehension Skills By Combining Writing With Collaborative Learning Activities–Fable Analysis and History examples

Description

Critical thinking skills can best be enhanced through a series of writing/collaborative learning exercises based upon specific course content. When students answer questions posed in the text individually and then compare their answers with a partner with the aim of formulating a combined response there are many aspects of critical thinking involved. Students arrive at their conclusions individually, communicate their answers to their partners verbally, listen to responses, which may be supportive or critical, discuss their partners comments, listen to their partner's oral presentation and respond orally or in writing, work with their partners to formulate a combined response or write a differing opinion if a consensus cannot be reached.

A major advantage to using this approach, especially as regards class discussion, is that many more students participate than in traditional class discussions where often only a few students (usually the same few) answer the teacher's questions. Also, in cases where students are shy or hesitant to speak out in class, or in cases involving difficult questions, a group answer provides a certain amount of "cover," for the answer truly does belong to the group and not just one individual. and responsibility for the answer is diffused throughout the group.

When structuring questions it is helpful to follow Bloom's taxonomy, moving from simpler comprehension questions that students can answer directly from the text/handout, to more difficult application, analysis and synthesis questions involving higher order thinking skills.

In the first part of this exercise typical textbook questions from a history lesson are reconfigured into writing assignments by developing worksheets. These may be completed for homework or in class as time permits. Additional space on the worksheet may be provided if more expansive answers are desired. The worksheets provide a mechanism for students to exchange their papers between group members. A single worksheet may be provided to the group to facilitate a collaborative response.

The first part of the exercise involves mainly information retrieval while the second and third parts use a higher level of critical thinking and analysis. Students are asked to identify and explain the significance behind an event, analyze a quotation and state both sides of an issue using a write and swap format. Part 3 extends student critical thinking skills further. Options are provided for possible use in a student portfolio or as a stand alone writing exercise. Various connections with civics, contemporary issues, writing, and time line analysis are used to form the basis for extended analysis and writing. Each of these assignments may be answered individually or using collaborative learning techniques.

Purposes

1. To enhance students critical thinking abilities through writing and collaborative learning activities.

2. To provide a range of critical thinking activities through a series of writing exercises which vary from information retrieval to analysis and opinion formation.

3. To provide writing exercises which would make good portfolio additions for students to demonstrate their work over time.

Alternate Uses

1. Students may be asked to make up their own set of questions for each of the sections and then answer them or exchange their questions within their groups.

2. A class discussion may follow the group interactions with teams or pairs presenting their combined responses in order to receive feedback from the whole class.

3. A booklet of responses may be created as a class project which focuses on a particular aspect of the course.

4. A class portfolio may be developed which uses the same question over time during the semester, such as time line development. Included in the portfolio would be the best responses from teams as determined by the class or the teacher.

Implications/Applications for Collaborative Learning Possibilities

1. This exercise is tailored to collaborative learning at each phase. The most effective grouping initially would be pairs for information retrieval. Larger groups would be applicable for the development of higher level critical thinking skills.

2. Teaching students group skills may be incorporated into these exercises. It is important for students to be trained in methods of reaching a consensus or presenting contradictory conclusions through minority reports or constructive criticism.

3. Groups may be used to brainstorm appropriate questions for the class to address in teams.

4. A Jig-Saw exercise may be used by assigning groups different questions. It then becomes each group's responsibility to convey their answers to the class in a manner they determine.

COMBINING READING SELECTIONS/ QUESTIONS/WRITING/CLASS DISCUSSION WITH COOPERATIVE LEARNING ACTIVITIES

- Organize the class into pairs or small groups (3 or 4).
- Assign a reading selection from the text or using a handout, one per pair. (If desired, the reading selection may be given as a homework assignment the previous evening, especially if the reading is a long one).
- Questions pertaining to the reading may be assigned from the text, if available, or developed by the teacher in the form of a worksheet questionnaire. A single worksheet is distributed to each group.

- The pair/group members discuss the questions among themselves and arrive at a consensus; the recorder writes down the group answers
- In cases where no consensus can be reached, the recorder lists conflicting opinions.
- All group members sign the worksheet when all questions are answered.
- When all groups have finished the work, the class comes together for discussion and review.
- The teacher calls on one member of a pair or group to read off the group's answers to a question, and can then include as many pairs/groups as desired to fully develop discussion around a question or as time permits. If several pairs /groups give a similar answer (for example, a simple question with a direct answer), the teacher can move ahead; with more complex questions involving higher level critical thinking skills and a variety of possible answers, the teacher may wish to elicit more ideas from a larger number of groups.
- When class discussion is complete, the teacher collects the worksheets from all pairs/groups.

COOPERATIVE EXERCISE FOR DEVELOPING COMPREHENSION SKILLS USING HISTORY EXAMPLES

Working in pairs answer each of the questions by forming an answer you can both agree on. Write your answers in complete sentences, not single words.

1) Why were colonies like Jamestown and Plymouth financed by joint-stock companies rather than private individuals?

2) What problems did the Jamestown settlers face?

3) How did John Smith help save Jamestown?

---

4) Why did the separatists journey to America?

5) How were the relations between the Plymouth settlers and the nearby Indians? Why?

6) Describe the conflict between the Puritans and King Charles I.

7) What agreement did the Massachusetts settlers think they had with god?

8) What values did the New England Way represent?

9) Why was there such a great demand for labor in the Chesapeake Tidewater?

10) Briefly describe the founding of:
    a) Maryland

    b) New Netherland

    c) New Jersey

    d) Pennsylvania

    e) The Carolinas

    f) Georgia

DEVELOPING CRITICAL THINKING AND WRITING SKILLS

WRITE YOUR ANSWER TO THE QUESTIONS AND THEN PASS YOUR PAPER TO YOUR PARTNER. YOUR PARTNER WILL WRITE THEIR REACTION AND COMMENTS ABOUT WHAT YOU WROTE AND RETURN THE PAPER. THEN YOU WILL DISCUSS EACH OTHER STORIES AND COMMENTS.

1) IDENTIFYING SIGNIFICANCE- What important idea was established after the Pilgrims landed outside the boundary of the Virginia Company's land in the Americas?

COMMENTS

2) ANALYZING A QUOTATION- John Smith's rule for the Jamestown colony was, "He that will not work neither shall he eat." Do you think this was a fair rule? Explain.

COMMENTS

3) STATING BOTH SIDES OF AN ISSUE- State (a) the argument that the governor of Massachusetts might have for banishing Roger Williams or Anne Hutchinson and (b) the reply those two might have given.

COMMENTS

PORTFOLIO OPTIONS–WORKING IN PAIRS ANSWER THE FOLLOWING QUESTIONS

1) CIVICS CONNECTION- Imagine that you and a group of colonists are settling in North America in the 1600's. Make up a government plan for your colony.

2) TIME LINE CONNECTION - Copy the chapter timeline. Which event do you think was most important?

time line—

3) Contemporary Connection - How, if at all, did the qualities and skills needed by the Jamestown settlers differ from those needed by settlers today?

4) WRITING CONNECTION - Support the following statement in a short essay: "By the early 1700's, the American colonies already contained a wide variety of peoples from different backgrounds.

6-ADDITIONAL SAMPLES OF WRITING ASSIGNMENTS

During the semester, in college courses, students in general will have particular difficulty understanding a concept. When this occurs it is helpful to ask the class as a whole to reflect upon their difficulties by writing about them. Their observations then may be shared in small groups and finally as a whole class discussion. This process often leads to students' having insights into their misunderstandings and generating suggestions about how to help themselves learn the material. Essentially any problem or question about course content or course procedures may be asked of the students and shared through cooperative activities and as whole class discussions.

The following are samples of writing assignments or group activities which have been developed for mathematics classes, which are intended to help students focus on difficult concepts. Only the exercise statements are presented in this section without additional explanation. They may be adapted to suit the needs of individual instructors or courses.

6A- 100% Success in Algebra
6B- Is The Mastery Approach To Testing A Good One???
6C- Math Anxiety Code of Responsibilities
6D- Mt Very Own Group's Strategy For Solving Word Problems
6E- Calculating Pi- Not The Kind You Eat- A Cooperative Exploration
6F- Why Are Fractional Exponents So Hard To Understand?
6G- Faculty Writing Exercise
6H- Developing a Preparation Strategy For Mastery Tests
6I- Solving Equations Together

100% SUCCESS IN ALGEBRA

Is it possible to have a completion rate of 100% in this class? This is the question I would like us to deal with over this semester. What incentives would motivate everyone to complete this class successfully? I have two thoughts/suggestions to start the discussion. These ideas are intended to provide some extrinsic motivation for us.

The underlying idea is to develop strategies which will encourage us to help each other, look after each other if we begin to falter or fall behind and provide a helping system for everyone in class. The suggestions I have are meant to be supportive, not punitive, i.e. if you do not take a final in a group but as a regular exam that would be no different than what we not do. If you get to do the final as a group that would be a great reward for excellent work during the semester.

I am looking for your ideas on things we might do to increase our motivation and help everyone pass this class with flying colors.

Ted's ideas

1) After about 3 weeks we will have formed permanent groups for the remainder of the semester. I would propose allowing any group whose members complete all the chapters at the 80% level to take the final exam as a group.

2) If the entire class completes the chapter tests at the 80% level or better then the final exam would be given as a take home test due back on the day of the final, instead of an in class final exam.

Your ideas

1)_____

2)_____.

Is The Mastery Approach To Testing A Good One???

"I know I can make corrections on the mastery if I make any mistakes, so I am not motivated to study for it."

"If I do not get 80% on the mastery I can retake it as many times as I need to. This means I don't need to study as much for the test."

These comments are typical of some responses I received from the writing assignments and in person from a few people. I am concerned that they may reflect a wider problem. I would like to find out if this is a problem. I would like your opinion on this approach to testing in algebra.

How do you feel about the mastery approach to testing in general? Does it increase or decrease your motivation to prepare for the mastery? Should I change this approach and go back to regular testing?

2. What can you do to help motivate yourself for the mastery or increase your readiness to demonstrate your mastery?

3. What can I (Ted) do to help motivate people for the mastery?

NAME _____

Math Anxiety Code of Responsibilities

by Kathy Acker

1. I have the responsibility to attend all classes and do all homework as assigned.

2. I have the responsibility to recognize the rights of others to learn at their own pace.

3. I have the responsibility to seek extra help when necessary.

4. I have the responsibility to see the teacher during office hours or to schedule an appointment for assistance.

5. I have the responsibility to come to class prepared; homework finished and/or questions to ask.

6. I have the responsibility to speak up when I don't understand.

7. I have the responsibility to give math at least the same effort I give to other subjects.

8. I have the responsibility to begin my math study at my current skill level.

9. I am responsible for my attitudes about my abilities.

10. I have the responsibility to learn about instructors prior to registering for class.

11. I have the responsibility for learning and practicing relaxation skills.

12. I have the responsibility to act as a competent adult.

13. I have the responsibility to approach math with an open mind rather than fighting it.

14. I have the responsibility to be realistic about my goals and expectations.

My Very Own Group's Strategy For Solving Word Problems

Using the individual strategies developed by each group member prior to class write up a strategy or process for solving word problems. What is the very first thing you do when starting to solve a word problem? What do you do next and so on.

Use the reverse side of this paper if necessary.

BE AS SPECIFIC AND DETAILED AS YOU CAN

_____
_____
_____
_____
_____
_____
_____
_____
_____
_____
_____
_____
_____
_____
_____
_____
_____
_____
_____

Name _____ Name _____

Name _____ Name _____

Calculating Pi—Not The Kind You Eat–A Cooperative Exploration

THIS EXERCISE IS INTENDED TO LET YOU EXPLORE THE CONCEPT OF PI BY WORKING WITH AT LEAST ONE OTHER PERSON IN YOUR GROUP OR IN THE CLASS. YOUR GROUP WILL DEVELOP DATA WHICH WILL HELP YOU UNDERSTAND HOW THE VALUE OF PI WAS DETERMINED AND HOW IT IS USED TO SOLVE AREA PROBLEMS

FIND SEVERAL ROUND OBJECTS IN YOUR HOME OR AT SCHOOL, SUCH AS A PLATE, COFFEE CUP, ROLL OF PAPER, ETC. YOU WILL NEED ENOUGH OBJECTS TO CONVINCE YOURSELF AND THE CLASS THAT YOUR CONCLUSION IS VALID

1) Sketch the circumference of each object on a piece of paper. Label each of the circles to identify which object it came from.

2) Measure around the circumference of each circle with a piece of string or tape measure. Note the distance under each circle.

3) Measure the diameter (across the circle defined by the object through the center) of each object and note the results under the previous measurement.

4) Divide the two measurements, part two divided by part 3.

5) Present your data in a form that can be easily understood by someone who is unfamiliar with the concept of Pi

6) What would you conclude about your results?

You are now ready to apply for a Nobel prize in algebra!

Why Are Fractional Exponents Hard To Remember And Workout???

While working on review problems for chapter 9 it became clear that something was missing. Even though we worked out quite a few problems from the text, prior to starting the review, there was unanimous confusion about how to simplify exponents where rational exponents are used. I have attached a review sheet dedicated to helping us practice simplifying fractional exponents. prior to completing this sheet I would like you to address two questions.

· 1. Why do you think you are having trouble working with and simplifying exponents where fractions are involved?

2. What ideas or approaches can you think of which will help you learn how to work with fractional exponents? I would like you to think of at least <u>three</u> things which you or your group or I can do to help everyone succeed in this section.

Idea 1

Idea 2

Idea 3

Group Summary- Question 1- Why are fractional exponents hard to learn?

Group Ideas to help us learn how to simplify fractional exponents.

Use the reverse side of the page if necessary.

Faculty Writing Assignment

At the last DE meeting we discovered that each of us deals with developmental students in different ways under the mastery approach. In order to help us understand the variety of approaches to mastery learning I would like to request that you answer the following questions prior to the next meeting on March 10th. I will compile the responses and distribute them prior to the meeting.

I am hopeful that we will be able to use this information to form a basis and rational for requests to the administration for additional support for the DE area, such as a re-test facility if that is what we decide is needed.

How do you handle students who do not pass your chapter tests on the first attempt?

How do you deal with your students' math anxiety?

Developing A Preparation Strategy For Mastery Tests

Your group is responsible for developing a set of strategies, guidelines, suggestions, approaches, etc. for helping each group member become prepared to complete the algebra masteries successfully. (Use the reverse side if needed)

1. What can you do personally to get ready for a chapter mastery?

2. What can we do in class to help us get ready for the masteries?

Name _____ Name _____

Name _____ Name _____

Solving Equations And Inequalities—Together

Name _____

Name _____

     Each partner will complete one step in the process of solving an equation then rewrite the remaining parts of the equation and pass the paper to their partner. Repeat the process until the equation is solved for the given variable.

     Show all your work clearly. Keep within the space provided and write neatly and legibly. Pass the paper in when you are finished.

1. $3(2X - 4) = 8$

2. $-2(4X - 5) = 7(X - 3)$

WAC Web Pages

Writing and Reading across the Curriculum Resources. Staff Development Workshops. Writing is Learning: Strategies for Math,. http://www.indiana.edu/~eric rec/bks/wac.html

Writing- and Communications-Across-the-Curriculum in the Materials Science and Engineering, Department at Virginia Tech. Robert W. Hendricks Eric Pappas. http://fre.www.ecn.purdue.edu/FrE/asee/fie95/4a4/4a43/4a43.html

Writing Across the Curriculum Links http://www.umsl.edu/~klein/WAC_links.html

LANDMARK ESSAYS ON WRITING ACROSS THE CURRICULUM. Volume 6 http://www.erlbaum.com/1604.htm

Writing Across the Curriculum assignments and writing samples. http://www.kcmetro.cc.mo.us/longview/wac/wachome.htm

The George Mason University Writing Across the Curriculum (WAC) Page. http://www.gmu.edu/departments/wac/

Purdue University Wac web site http://owl.english.purdue.edu/

http://www.english.uiuc.edu/cws/wworkshop/

WAC in Community Colleges

Kirkwood Community College (Cedar Rapids, Iowa)
http://www.kirkwood.cc.ia.us/english/wac/wacpage.htm

Chabot College (Hayward, California) (contact Dennis Chowenhill)
http://la.clpccd.cc.ca.us/wrac/
Kapiolani Community College (Hawaii)
http://leahi.kcc.hawaii.edu/pub/intersect/wac.html

Longview Community College (Kansas City, MO)
http://www.kcmetro.cc.mo.us/longview/wac/wachome.htm

St. Louis Community College
http://www.stlcc.cc.mo.us/fvdocs/wac/

WAC/CAC/ECAC bibliographies.

The LALAC Bibliography,
http://www.sfasu.edu/lalac/bibliog.html

Indiana University at Bloomington's Annotated WAC Bibliography,
http://www.indiana.edu/~wts/cwp/lib/
wacgen.html#wacgen.lltml

SUNY at Cortland's WAC Guide for Faculty,
http://orchard.cortland.edu/wac.htm

ERIC Bibliography on WAC in Secondary Schools,
http://www.indiana.edu/~eric rec/ieo/bibs/wac-sec.html

Georgia State University's Discipline-Specific WAC Bibliographies,
http://WWW.GSU.EDU/~wwwwac/

Learning Together